To
Lynn

a Butterfly 🦋

Energy

love ya!

Rock

D1369939

THE POWER OF
YOUR IDENTITY

ROCK THOMAS

Bloomington, IN Milton Keynes, UK

AuthorHouse™
1663 Liberty Drive, Suite 200
Bloomington, IN 47403
www.authorhouse.com
Phone: 1-800-839-8640

AuthorHouse™ UK Ltd.
500 Avebury Boulevard
Central Milton Keynes, MK9 2BE
www.authorhouse.co.uk
Phone: 08001974150

First published by AuthorHouse 12/15/2006

ISBN: 978-1-4259-8270-6 (sc)

Library of Congress Control Number: 2006910514

Printed in the United States of America
Bloomington, Indiana

This book is printed on acid-free paper.

Dedicated to all those people who want more but feel that they can't find their way out of what they keep on doing. To those that feel stuck on the merry-go-round of life, but want more – here is the recipe that worked for me!

To my mother for her example of being someone who lives in the moment and with enthusiasm!

To my father whose words seem wiser with each passing day. May his soul rest in peace.

Acknowledgements

I would like to thank all those who helped me make this book a reality.

To my wife Lisa, who encouraged and inspired me with her words and by being a role model to me.

To my best friend Mark, for giving me the leverage to set a deadline or to run another marathon.

To my kids, for being my teachers and examples for this book.

To Aalia Persaud, my editor and personal assistant, who endured dozens of revisions yet stayed positive and enthusiastic all the way.

To Pamela Jay, my publisher.

The Power of Your Identity

Acknowledgements

Preface

Chapter 1: Who Are You? Can You Change?

Preface

How many books claim to hold the winning formula for change? You've heard it before: set goals, dream big, take action, overcome your fears, you can do it, attitude is everything... blah, blah, blah. What makes this book different? It is uniquely different in that it takes you to the core — no more surface and symbolic changes. Deep below the surface of the earth is where you find gold and diamonds. The same goes for your potential. So take the plunge with me into the center of how you have been shaped. It is now time to rejuvenate your identity. You deserve the best and you will get it.

Surely you've observed how successful people have **characteristics and habits** they repeat consistently. People like Tiger Woods, Claude Lemieux, Michael Jordan, Wayne Gretkzy, Donald Trump, Anthony Robbins and Bill Gates have similar characteristics and habits. **We aren't born successful nor are we born failures – we learn one or the other.** The good news is that we can switch. To me, failure means living your life without fulfillment, without happiness and without obtaining your desired goals.

Mike Tyson has had fame and made millions of dollars, yet he is an emotionally tormented man. This book is about getting you to the next level of fulfillment and achievement in all areas of your life. Please imagine for a moment that you could choose to be whoever you'd like to be with whatever habits, beliefs or traits that you desire. Most of us have picked up some habits that are not working so well. You may have been making tremendous effort and still sometimes feel that success is reserved for others. Or perhaps, like I have, you achieved a modicum of success in your career but you are emotionally tired and stressed and not taking care of your body. Later on

I will walk you through a menu of successful characteristics, one by one, so you will start to see how **simple** success really is. That does not mean it is without effort. It means that there's a way: *A recipe to results.*

The Peak Performance Formula

These characteristics, once implemented in your life with consistency, will allow you to obtain any result you desire. The key is "desire." In fact, it will have to be a burning desire. Isn't it true that we live in a "try" society? People who say, "I'll try!" I recently promoted an employee to vice-president of one of my companies, based upon the fact that he never says "I'll try." Whenever he is given a task, his response is "consider it done!" Now doesn't that sound a lot better? It sure does to me!

I encourage you to do the exercises in this book. They will assist you with getting results that last. Confucius once said "I hear and I forget. I see and I believe. I do and I understand." Please feel free to read this book again and again. Repetition is what conditions your unconscious mind to get results effortlessly. *Repetition is the skill of success.* I'm asking you to put the effort in early so your unconscious mind will do it for you automatically. Each characteristic of success is like an ingredient in a delicious cake. If you are missing any one ingredient, your chances of success will decrease.

Seeing people frustrated, overwhelmed, discouraged and living life trying to avoid pain, has been a great motivator for me to write this book. You see, things will not get better until you put in the effort. You must obtain the essence of success and apply it at a level that is better than what you are currently employing! **You need to be the one who will set the standard for your results.**

You are either living your dream or you are missing it! In this book you will learn how to energize that dream, refuel you desires, fire up your relationships and your career, and feel more energetic than ever.

Your dream, that burning desire, is the part of you that makes you feel so alive! Whether it be for singing, dancing, acting, becoming a doctor, nurse or fireman, **that is the part of you that resonates within your body and makes you come alive! It is your reason for being! It's your <u>M</u>ission, your <u>V</u>ision and your <u>P</u>urpose. It's what I call your:**

MVP

In order to evolve and improve, we need to first become aware of our circumstances. Then, equipped with this awareness, we make our plan. Finally, we implement the plan by getting leverage on ourselves — commonly referred to as being motivated. By following these steps, we achieve our desired result.

Each chapter of this book is broken into steps to help you achieve the results you desire:

Chapter 1 — Developing your awareness for who you are and how you can change!

Chapter 2 — Deciding who you really want to be and how to be your best through your Mission, Vision and Purpose (MVP).

Chapter 3 — How to develop your Identity — in writing.

Chapter 4 — Closing the Gap: How to spend time with your optimal self.

Chapter 1:
Who Are You? Can You Change?

Success is the ability to experience failure with out losing enthusiasm.
— **Winston Churchill**

What do we all want?

1) To change or modify our behavior

2) To live in better emotional states

What habit are you trying to change? Which habit would you like to have? Perhaps you are trying to quit smoking, eat less or would like to follow through more consistently. Or maybe you would like to improve your golf game, enhance your negotiation techniques or become a better lover?

My goal is to get a detailed look at who you are. The way to do this is to establish who you have become based upon all of the influences in your life: the people who have affected your life and the events in your life that have caused you to be fearful or open to new things. You've been shaped in one way or another and now parts of that are serving you and parts are enslaving you. It's time to get knowledgeable. **<u>Who are you?</u>** Write it down in detail. In so doing, you will discover the parts of you that are holding you back from getting the results that you want in your life.

What Do You Value?

Once you've described who you are, the next part will be for you to ask yourself: **<u>What is important to me in my life</u>**? What is important to you are the things that you value. Maybe you love to have freedom and peace, adventure or the pressure of responsibility. These are the emotional states that you value, the ones that give you pleasurable feelings.

Become familiar with your identity. This will allow you to make decisions and to make them quickly and easily. All of the decisions you make each and every day will continue to shape your identity. You'll never be really happy unless you're growing. Staying who you are today forever will not bring you happiness. Just as a child enjoys watching the progress of a puppy growing every day, so do we yearn for our own growth.

Regardless of what result you desire to create, you will have to address yourself at a "core" level or you will **not** achieve lasting change. How many people do you know that have started yet another diet only to end up back where they were or worse? How many of us are stressed at work because of the changes that society brings or the difficulty we have with adapting to continuous change? How many of us live in fear of losing our job or of being left by our mate? In essence, people from all over the world have a fear of not being enough. We go through our days trying to find ways to overcome this daunting and haunting fear.

For years, I tried and tried to get better results in my life, working harder and longer, taking massive action, only to fall back to where I was. Each time I felt more frustrated, more disappointed and more discouraged. My response was to develop coping habits.

Coping Habits
Overeating, drinking, smoking, passive aggressive behavior, self-pity, bursts of anger, justification and rationalization stories to back up unloving and uncaring behavior.

When I hit rock bottom, my search took a turn for the better. We have all heard the statement "one day you will laugh about this" or "your toughest day will one day be a blessing and a turning point in your life." These statements are true. At the time it may be difficult to understand but once you get through it, you grow stronger and you will have that strength to bring with you to the next fight. As long as you keep on picking yourself up off the mat, you will <u>start to win</u>.

The Power Of Your Identity

I discovered that there were people who were getting the results they desired on their terms! In spite of all the obstacles, I began a quest to discover and learn their skills. At the heart of the matter is what we call our "identity." This is the way that you see yourself; **the way you believe** you should behave and how others expect you to behave. The internal memory you have about **who you are** and how you are supposed to behave will dictate your future behavior. Your identity will lead you to all of your actions. Your actions, once stored as memories, have a huge impact on how you feel. When they are repeated, your actions become your habits and thus part of your identity.

This is a book about expanding your identity! Your identity is the "father of your actions." Everything that you DO will be determined by how you describe yourself or how you see yourself – thus creating a persona or IDENTITY. That means that YOUR IDENTITY can either empower you or disempower you. It will prevent or compel you to take certain actions.

Your behavior will be consistent with the image that you hold of yourself. It becomes your unconscious guide. Your desire to remain congruent with your identity is a powerful force that left unmanaged, will manipulate your life out of control forever!

— Rock Thomas

One of the most important acts you perform in your life will be to define who YOU are! Fail to do this, and you will become a constellation of other people's wishes, fears and desires. When you are growing up, the images that you attach emotions to shape how you see yourself and how you feel about yourself. Our minds easily grasp life's lessons through the example of metaphors. We tend to link things we *know* to what we *don't know* more easily than we link an unknown to the unknown. I will use the metaphors of the "Garden of Life" to describe your Identity, "The Ship" for your unconscious mind and the "Captain" for your conscious mind.

The Garden Of Life

Imagine that your identity — the way that you see yourself and others see you — is like a garden. Imagine that there are eight plots and each one represents an area of your life. They are: **Emotions, Spiritual, Family and Friends, Intimate Relationships, Career, Financial, Hobbies** and **Health**.

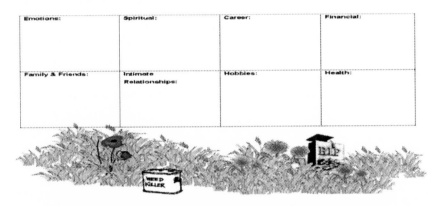

Emotions:	Spiritual:	Career:	Financial:
Family & Friends:	Intimate Relationships:	Hobbies:	Health:

With each plot you will have a history or His-story/Her-story. The weeds will represent negativity and the trees and flowers will represent success, wealth, health, happiness and all that we desire in life. Some areas may be doing better than others, but why? It all comes down to what we focus on in our lives!

The Captain And His Crew

There are two parts to your brain: one is the conscious (the Captain) and the other is the unconscious (your Crew). Imagine that you are the Captain and you can give orders to your Crew at anytime and they are happy to carry them out. In fact, this is what they live for. They do not question your orders, they take them at face value and they get better and better each time. The more you get them to do the same thing, the more they crave that activity themselves. Orders that are given with uncertainty will be carried out that way. Orders that are wishy-washy will often get forgotten or muddled. Conversely, any orders that are stated with certainty will also be carried out that way. Your crew simply follows and mirrors what the captain thinks or says. The communication that will take place between the Captain (your conscious mind) and his/her Crew (your unconscious) will be a common theme through out this book.

Think about when you graduated from high school and your yearbook had a picture with a description below you. Based upon your past behavior, someone gave you a description that was meant to predict your future behavior. Well, today you have a description of this (identity) in your mind and whenever you think about doing something, your conscious mind verifies what is stored in your memory (in the unconscious) and these internal references and pictures of the past I call **your identity**.

Your mind's goal is to see if there is a match— if that is how you have behaved in the past — and whether or not you should be repeating that same behavior. Typically when someone feels that there is no prior history of that behavior, they respond by saying, "No, that is not me." We hear that all the time. For instance, if you were to ask someone "Would like to go skiing?", if they are not a skier, how will they respond? "Which hill are you going to?" No, of course not! They would say, "No thanks. I AM NOT A SKIER." You see, we determine our behavior as something we are or something that we are not. I believe our environment affects us all. Being in a negative one causes most people to mute their dreams and to live their lives trying to avoid pain. People will always do more to avoid pain than they will to gain pleasure. People will do more to avoid the "fear of pain" than to pursue joy or happiness!

Triple E™

What we attach pain and pleasure to will vary greatly from person to person. How you are is determined by your emotional experiences, especially those that were extreme. Those extreme emotions shaped your values, your beliefs, and what you feel is right or wrong. Strong role models and Extreme Emotional Experiences (Triple E™) are a primary force in determining your pain and pleasure filters.

Acne Shaped His Self-Image

As a teenager I experienced very strong emotions when it came to my self-image, specifically because of severe acne. There were days when I would not go outside because I had a big pimple on my face. I would wish for the day that I would no longer have them and that others would look at me differently. When I discovered that the sun would help my skin clear up, I became addicted to suntanning. Wanting so badly to not endure the humiliation from my acne, I decided to move to Australia where it is sunny and warm almost all year around. My goal was to reduce the pain that I felt by changing the way I saw myself so that others would be attracted to me. I tried all kinds of creams and external ways to change an internal feeling and self-perception. I began to drink to numb the pain that I was feeling from not having the look that I wanted.

Not knowing how to achieve a positive inner mindset, I **chose** to focus on the outer world to change how I felt. Using drinking as part of my strategy backfired, because the more sugar I put into my body in the form of alcohol, the worse my acne became. I did not know this, but the numbing of my emotions (reducing the feelings of loneliness and rejection) kept me on the drinking trail. Seeking further relief from my pimply self-image I fled to Southeast Asia to be among people I did not know. I was trying to hide what made me feel bad. I often felt sad and wondered who would look beyond these pimples and really want me for who I was? Why did it have to happen to me? For many years, the first thing I would do every day when I woke up would be to go to the bathroom mirror hoping that there would be no new pimples from the past night's sleep. The shock and horror when a new one would appear was very painful. My dilemma became: hide it or hide me?

These thoughts occupied my mind continually, day in and day out. I was preoccupied thinking "Is someone looking? What are they thinking?" Pain and more pain coursed through my veins! Our unconscious minds (our Crew) are always looking for a way out of pain for us. This is a good thing except when we lack the resources or the skills to achieve this ecologically. So, I would go to tanning salons knowing that it could be harmful to expose my skin to these lamps; I still chose to do so in hopes of clearing the skin to remove the acne so that I could feel better and feel attractive to others.

Our identities are like bank accounts. We can only withdraw what has been deposited. Your identity is formed when you deposit experiences, and during the course of your life you withdraw them, solidifying who you are the more you do any one act. Some are negative and some are positive. When we say the phrase "**I am**" followed by another word, for instance: lazy, fat, smart, funny, wise, stupid, adventurous, shy, uncoordinated, too small, too young, too old – these are direct descriptions of how we see ourselves and how we feel we should perform or behave.

Your ability to process failure and to attach empowering meanings when getting a negative result is crucial to your long-term success. Your transformation from a person who avoids life to a person who embraces life and all of its colorful

7

emotions will be in direct proportion to your ability to see the positive (or the gift) in all that you do or in what occurs in your life.

Nothing has meaning but the meaning we attach to it. By developing the skill to persistently and consistently look for and find the GREAT in all things, you will fill your identity's inventory (the unconscious) with the highest level of behavior possible. The most successful people in the world do not have fewer bad things happen to them. They simply have a more robust inventory of behavior options to select their actions from, leading them to the best possible paths and/or results. This creates a positive self-image or a positive identity. This will also feed your self-esteem and encourage self-confidence. Otherwise, you will tend to spiral down when what you do is stored as a disempowering event. That disempowering event will inevitably be withdrawn later to strengthen your negative self-image.

Learning to give a positive meaning to all that happens to you increases your positive inventory.

1. Oprah Winfrey was born in the 1950s. She was poor, black and a girl. She was raped as a child. She chose to become a strong woman who could advocate and help the underprivileged and abused. She created a powerful and meaningful life for herself.

2. MADD (Mothers Against Drunk Driving). These women, many whose lives have been personally affected by drunk drivers, make a difference by campaigning and saving the lives of thousands with their message.

3. Terry Fox had bone cancer and one leg amputated six inches above his knee. He began the cross-Canada *Marathon of Hope* to raise money for cancer research. His legacy and marathon continue to live on in the hearts of Canadians and others throughout the world, showing that anything is possible with a dream.

Nothing has meaning until you determine and attach a meaning to it. You are the master of your own meanings. This single tool has the power to change your entire life from that of a victim to a victor.

How do you go from where you are to where you want to be? I think you have to have an enthusiasm for life. You have to have a dream, a goal and you have to be willing to work for it.

— **Jim Valvano**

Re-Framing

Each time you feel yourself about to attach a negative meaning to something that has happened, imagine the best. Pretend you're in a contest to come up with the most positive meaning. Remember that you have choices in life. One of the most powerful choices that you have is what **meaning** you will attach to everything that happens to you. Will you deposit that event into your bank as a "negative" or a "positive" event? Remember, that once deposited as "negative" or "positive", you will withdraw it for future use from the same account that you placed it into.

Example: You get fired. Most people would say that's negative. What could you say to yourself?
- There is a better job waiting for me.
- I needed the push to open my own business, now I can do it.
- I really didn't like that job, I'm just being helped to move on to something more fulfilling. Yippee!
- New opportunities are waiting for me now!

Example: You have a fender-bender. What could you say to yourself?
- Be more careful and less preoccupied.
- It could have been worse — thank goodness it wasn't.
- I can afford to pay the repairs — good.
- I just created a job for someone — yippee!

The meanings you attach to things are abundantly free. Your imagination is the only thing that limits you. Be a child again. Find the best meanings and plug them into each event. Transform the meanings in your life, transform the quality of your emotions and live in the garden of your own creativity — the Garden of Eden.

Example: Your doctor tells you some bad news about your health.

- You can do something right away to improve it by being responsible and not becoming a victim.
- It could have gone on undetected. Now you can deal with it.
- You can afford it. You live in a great country.
- You have friends to help you through it.

Your mindset evolves from your inner dialogue or self-talk. Choose your self-talk wisely and empower yourself to a full, fantastic, fulfilling life. You can shape and influence events, yet there are many outside events you cannot control. But what you can control is the "meaning" that you attribute to or attach to them BEFORE you deposit them into the bank account of your identity.

Sally was six years old when her brother told her to stop singing, because it was hurting his ears. She loved to sing, but she felt ashamed and embarrassed. For years she sang only when she was alone. She became a teacher, yet at the age of 38 she still felt unfulfilled. Finally, listening to her inner voice, she took singing lessons and performed at the local talent show. She now sings every week. A whole new world has opened up and she feels better in all areas of her life.

Your genius or magic will emerge when you find your "Context of Purpose." For Tiger Woods it is the golf course. For Oprah it is television. For Jim Carey it is entertainment. For Celine Dion it is singing. For Wayne Gretzky it is hockey. For Bill Gates it is computers!

What is your purpose? What is the purpose of your being here? Most people don't know what they want. There is no way for you to purposely go toward a target if you haven't set that target in advance. We'll be talking about goal-setting in order for you to understand its value and why it is so instrumental in your success strategy. Discovering the context of your purpose or the arena where you'll shine is paramount to fulfillment.

MVP: Mission, Vision, Purpose

Mission: *Short-term goals that lead to your ultimate purpose.*
Vision: *How you see your life once it's completed.*
Purpose: *Your "why" – your fuel, your reason.*

This book is about **creating a compelling desire to make a difference in your life and to live your dream.** This book will teach you to be your personal best; to feel, to think about, talk about, tell others, define and redefine your MVP. That is the map. If you do not create your map, you will always feel lost and off course. You will need to invest some time defining what you truly are here to offer, or what is your life assignment so your genius can emerge!

On some level, many people have a burning desire to make a difference. Yet their purpose has been beaten down by the disappointments of life (the negative or disempowering meanings they attached to past events). Thus, they have given up on their dream. They keep telling themselves that they don't know what they want anymore. Then, when somebody says, "Do you want this?" They reply, "I don't know." They have virtually hypnotized themselves into a state of not knowing. They just react to their environment. **It's only when conditions force them to step up that they step up.** When a drastic event happens — divorce, death, illness — they are forced to dig down and find the answers using their otherwise untapped potential. Was it always there? Yes it was! Why have they not acted upon it? The answer is that people don't lack desires.

11

They lack the reasons (motivation) to overcome the obstacles that clarity of purpose brings to the forefront.

Life Determines Your Life Path If You Don't

Example: Suppose you can't pay your mortgage, Visa or MasterCard bill. With your back to wall, you are compelled to take on a second job or to work overtime, so you do. **If you're going to wait until life tells you what to do, you're never going to feel that you're creating your own path.** In other words, you're stuck in your comfort zone, bouncing around from one menial task or relationship to another. You're in the zone of distraction trying to watch TV, eat and consume products that are going to numb the pain of not being associated to your purpose. You've got to have a purpose and be connected to it in order to get the juices flowing. The drive necessary to carry on through life's obstacles comes from **clarity of purpose**.

All successful people, men and women, are big dreamers. They imagine what their future could be, ideal in every respect, and then they work every day toward their distant vision, that goal or purpose.

— Brian Tracy

People from every culture and country share an innate drive for meaning, direction and purpose. This craving to know our path and life purpose seems as important to our psychological needs of fulfillment as oxygen is to our daily needs for physical survival. The moment we connect with our life's purpose, it will be like a fog lifting from our once vague lives. The mundane day-to-day tasks of doing our jobs, raising our children, problem solving and fighting the obstacles to make our lives less painful will all seem to change. Change insofar as they are not random meaningless events, but rather parts of a whole. As you gain hold of your purpose, time will disappear and the sun will shine even on rainy days causing you to align with your innermost talents and revealing abilities that you never even knew existed.

The Power Of Questions

By formulating a question that will give us the answer we want, we empower ourselves! Ask yourself, "What would I do if I knew I could not fail?" Really, what would it be? **There is power in purpose**, who you are today and how you can expand that will become clear through the proper use of questions.

If you're not sure what your purpose is, you're not alone. **About 95% of people don't have an overall clear purpose for their life.**[1] They lack meaning and therefore they lack drive! They end up getting the leftovers from somebody else's purpose. They get plugged into the minor role that helps someone else achieve their dream (purpose). It doesn't mean you have to create world peace or that you have to go to Africa and feed the hungry. The benefit of living your life's purpose is that it necessitates your alignment with the universal laws of success. These are principles that you respect at the unconscious level. These principles affect all of us.

These laws or principles are not merely suggestions or codes of ethical conduct. They express our innermost desires to honor a higher self in our society. We may attempt to ignore gravity, but it will not ignore us. A law or a principle does not care if we respect it; its innate structure will impose itself upon us. These principles are time-tested and true. That's why we call them principles. Those who succeed in getting outstanding results in life seek to understand these forces, knowing they will be exerted upon them. The application of these principles doesn't depend upon any kind of belief on your behalf — gravity works whether you believe in it or not. However, once you embrace your life's purpose, these principals become a natural part of your tool kit. Their power will assist you in governing your focus, your choices and your decisions.

---

[1] Napoleon Hill.

Starting out to make money is the greatest mistake in life. Do what you feel you have a flair for doing, and if you are good enough at it, the money will come.

— Greer Garson

What does your **comfort zone** mean? Many people say, well, I'm not comfortable with this or that. What does that mean? Could it be possible that your comfort zone is something that helps you decide in advance where your boundaries are, thus making it easy for you to make your decisions? If you say that "I'm not somebody who bowls, knits or white water rafts," doesn't it then make it easy when somebody asks you to bowl, knit or white water raft? You need only check in with "who you are" and then say yes or no. In this case you say, "That's not me, I don't do those things." **Your identity or comfort zone predetermines what you've done and what you're apt to do in the future**.

The caliber of questions you ask yourself will lead to the caliber of the answers you get from yourself. Any good lawyer knows that the better the questions, the better he directs his witness to give the right answer. I would like for you to consider yourself in a like manner, where if you ask yourself the right question, you'll get the right answer. Imagine what answer you would like yourself to have if you were cross-examining yourself for success. Our brain will produce an answer to every question we ask of it. Often we answer "I don't know," yet that is really just a bad pattern of response or a reflex. The key to success is in having a plethora of great questions to ask ourselves for different contextual situations.

Power questions — questions for different situations.

Catalyst Questions:

o   What am I excited about?

o   What do I love in my life?

o   What am I passionate about?

o   What am I going to focus on today?

o   What am I going to do that brings me closer to my MVP?

o   Who am I going to be a role model for?

o   What are the most important things I need to do this week? This day? This month? This year?

o   How can I make today the most enjoyable?

o   What do I really want to do?

o   How do I want to feel?

o   What's the best thing I can do to get the most out of my life?

o   How can I empower others around me?

o   How can I add value today to my business, my family, my environment?

o   How can I be the very best me?

o   How can I nourish my body today to make it even healthier?

o   How can I support those in my life, in my environment?

o   What can I do today for somebody I don't even know?

o   How can I pay it forward today?

o   What is my greatest strength?

o   What do I love about myself?

o   What am I most grateful for?

o   What do I love about my family — my children, my relatives?

o   How can I show this gratitude even more in this moment?

My Favorite Challenge Question:

o   What's great about this?

Other versions of this:

o   What's not perfect yet?

o   How can I make this better?

o   What am I willing to do right now to turn this around?

o   How can I make the best of this situation?

o   How can I learn from this situation?

o   What can I learn from this situation?

o   What is the hidden gift in this situation?

o   What am I going to pull from this opportunity?

o   Who can help me with this situation? What resources do I need to draw upon?

o   When did I overcome a situation similar to this and succeed?

It is really important at the end of the day to have some questions that you can ask yourself in order to focus on the joy of each day.

o   What am I grateful for?

o   What did I learn?

o   What did I contribute?

o   How did I make a difference?

o   What were the highlights of my day?

o   What made me laugh?

o   What made me feel deeply and emotional?

o   How was I a good role model?

o   Where did I push myself to grow?

o   What are a few things that I want to be grateful for and to think about while I sleep tonight?

Various other questions:
- Who do I love to spend time with?
- What is supremely important to those who are most important to me?
- What's the most important thing I should be doing today?
- What's an area of my life that I want to focus on and make better? What am I willing to do about it?
- When am I at my best?
- How much more do I love myself today than I did yesterday?
- How can I make the most out of this moment in my life?
- How can I best serve today?
- How can I empower others? How can I show others that there is a better way?
- How can I be the change that I wish to see in the world?
- How much will it mean to me in the future to say "no" to this today?
- How much will it mean to me in the future to say "yes" to this today?

Start With A Charge

When you get up in the morning, in order to set the tone of the day, you'll note that I have a series of catalyst questions that will direct your focus to things that are going to make you feel and act in a resourceful and powerful way. Behaving in a way that's going to get you the results you want will make all the difference in the world.

Many people struggle to wake up in the morning and tend to take a little time to get the motor running. They get their coffee and they put on the radio or grab the paper after trying to wake up in the shower and get the cobwebs out. Imagine you get up in the morning and get into the shower where you focus on the wall to find your six or eight favorite questions that you could choose from to direct your focus. Remember: what you focus on becomes your reality and will direct your behavior.

One of the most powerful ways to create focus is through the power of questions. Ask these questions consistently if you want to expand your self-image into somebody who is directed and focused from the moment they wake up. For example:

- What am I grateful for?
- What I am excited about?
- What I am happy about?
- What I am passionate about?
- What can I do today that will take me closer to my dreams?
- Who is in my life that I love?

By peppering yourself with questions such as what you are excited, happy or passionate about, you will find yourself focusing on an inviting future, an exciting day and being energized by what is possible. It engages your imagination rather than leaving space for you to worry.

Because of the negative nature of the media, we tend to be directed by radio, TV and newspapers and exposed to all the negative in the world. It requires a daily strategy to enable us to overcome the hypnosis that is regularly offered by our culture. You will either choose your thoughts and dreams or society will give you what it thinks you should focus on. Our brains are so powerful that we must take control. We must direct what our sensitive "hard drives" absorb and make them quality thoughts, beliefs and values to assist ourselves in building a strong self-image/identity.

Those are some basic questions for the morning to kick-start your focus. You see, things are going to happen throughout the day that will stink! There will be obstacles as we set ourselves on a path towards rich results. And so the tests begin. We know that we have chosen to have a worthy opponent and a worthy goal or destination. So we begin to sculpt our self-concept. Doing so means we are in the process of preparation. That preparation must be met with an outstanding mindset, which will allow us to show up with the maximum possible resources: the best part of ourselves.

Transforming Problems Into Opportunities

When bad things happen, the very first question I suggest you ask yourself is: "What's great about this?" Or you could ask "What's not perfect about this?" followed by, "What's the lesson here? What's the gift?" If you ask those questions habitually with each and every obstacle that comes your way, you're going to find that you get better and better at coming up with outstanding answers. You may be clumsy at it at first. You may not even believe it at first. As you ask yourself, "What's great about this?" your reflexive answer might be "There is nothing great about this. This sucks." But practice. Hang in there. Our unconscious minds respond to repetition. The scientific reason lies in that connections are made between your neurons. The ability for you to replicate a behavior or recall information is greatly enhanced when these neuron connections are strengthened through repetition.

Your Neurology: Is It Positive Or Negative?

Use caution for every negative reaction or you might develop a negative neurology though habit. This explains why addictions are so hard to give up. The cells in your body literally take on a memory that has a chemical addiction to it. An addiction is something you cannot control! So, if you cannot control anger, fear or worry, your cells have become chemically addicted to those behaviors that you have conditioned through repetition.

Successful people don't have any less challenge than you or I. What they do is they have the ability to snap out of a negative mindset more rapidly than other people. They receive the information from an event just like you or I do. Then they create the internal picture that best suits them to show up in the best possible way. People often try to control events rather than learning skills to control the controllable. The controllable is actually their reaction to the event. By asking "What action can I take right now to make this better? To make it the way I want it?" would be a high calibre question for handling obstacles.

Hint: We hear people complaining every day about things that they (or even others) can't control. They complain about the weather or the amount of taxes they pay. Pretty soon they develop "pity partners" and unofficial support groups for feeling bad. Telling your neighbour about the bad parking spot at the office or sharing your financial woes with someone who has worse money problems than you won't benefit either party. Remember that challenges will always show up in your day. Either you treat them consistently with a strategy that works or you do so randomly and hope for the best! By asking a better question – "What's great about this?" – you control your focus and improve your ability to be resourceful.

Make Your Own Highlight Reel
At The End Of The Day

Finally, we want to catch the highlights of our day. When we condition ourselves to recall the best moments and feel great about them, we increase our own self-esteem. All too often we focus on the negatives of our day and brush off the funny moments and downplay our own successes, letting them fade into the bedlam of our memories.

Make it a practice to write in your journal. As you journal, you actually reinforce in your memory bank the items that are going to make you feel good about yourself. **If you only focus on the missed opportunities, the bad presentations and your clumsy moments, your self-esteem is going to go down** and you're going to start spiralling backwards into fear and inaction. You won't move toward your dreams. Instead, you'll move away from pain.

MVP

The biggest mistake people make in life is not trying to make a living at doing what they most enjoy. Success follows doing what you want to do. There is no other way to be successful.
— **Malcolm S. Forbes**

I want you to imagine a circle, any size. This represents your comfort zone. The purpose of your life lies within your ability to expand that comfort zone. If we were to agree that living equals growth — expanding and multiplying — if that's the general purpose of our life, then our goal is to find the best possible strategy to enlarge that comfort zone.

See yourself in that circle, wanting to expand it. How you get outside of that comfort zone is crucial to your being extremely emotionally associated to the purpose in your life. Being connected to your MVP will give you the juice, passion and motivation to overcome any and all obstacles that are going to come up once you've set your plan in motion. Think of Martin Luther King, Ghandi, Nelson Mandela, Helen Keller, Amelia Earhart, Tiger Woods or Oprah. They had or have all connected themselves with a role that defines or defined their direction daily.

Face Your Fear And It Will Disappear

When she was nine, my daughter wanted to jump off the diving board into the pool. Yet it was outside of her comfort zone (meaning her identity had no reference that said "I've done that"). She said, "Daddy, I don't want to do it. I'm afraid."

"Sweetheart, your sister did it. She's one year younger than you. She gets so much pleasure from it. Can you see her going? Look, watch her go," I replied. As she watched, she would see the joy, the pleasure and the payoff. It compelled her to step outside of her comfort zone and try it for herself.

With faith, courage and certainty (which are the emotions that I believe come before you gain confidence) she was able to do it. Once she did it, she didn't want to stop. The rest of the day, she was jumping and saying, "Look, Daddy!" and telling me how much fun it was. Then she asked me, "Daddy, why didn't you have me do it two weeks ago?" No longer attached to her old identity, she now expanded how she saw herself and embraced the joy of her newfound comfort zone and new identity.

Joy and happiness lie within the realm of uncertainty. Your ability to get yourself to act in spite of the fear of the unknown will determine the quality of your life. The fact of the matter is that what's on the outside of your comfort zone equals growth, and that means you must face those fears in order to grow. Fear is natural and something that we all experience. It's good that our antennaes go up to warn us of potential pain, otherwise we would be hurting ourselves unnecessarily. Fear can serve you. There is a gift in fear. Still, we must find a way to come up with a strategy to get us outside of our comfort zone and to explore the things that align us with our MVP. There is obviously no sense in skydiving if we will have a nervous breakdown. Nor should we become an accountant if numbers are tedious for us. I'm talking about doing things that bring us closer to our MVP — our dream. I'm talking about the need to know what you value and where that comes from.

Remaining in your comfort zone is like being stuck. If you spend the rest of your life doing what you're already doing, you risk boredom. You will be miserable. You've seen people who live their lives in their comfort zones. They're just doing the same thing they did yesterday. When that gets boring, they may unconsciously create problems in their lives to add some excitement. What I'm talking about is creating a specific strategy for success that allows you **to feel confident without having had the experience**.

How cool would it be to just decide "Hey, I want to ride motorcycles and skydive"? Or maybe open a new business, walk across the room and ask a girl or a guy out on a date. I'm talking about feeling confident, courageous and certain that you can do it.

Fear is a major blockage in the arteries of success. Fear of embarrassment holds people back from trying new things. (This explains why many people sing in their cars or in the shower.)

Every great movement must experience three stages: ridicule, discussion, adoption.

— **John Stuart Mill**

People have associated change to the famous four-letter word: **fear**. Fear is really the unknown and the uncertainty that something new is going to make you step outside of what you know – and therefore might mean pain. Here's a way that you can become attracted to uncertainty: become addicted to the unknown, release the chains of fear and embrace the new – just as my daughter did by jumping off the diving board.

Elephants are trained and conditioned to live within a zone. They can move within that zone by limiting their behavior with a strong chain (later to become a belief) from a young age. Later, no more than a small string will keep them from breaking free. This is based on repeated conditioning and thus instills the limiting belief that they cannot move beyond the rope. What limiting beliefs have been installed in your life that are now but tiny strings holding you back from expanding beyond your comfort zone?

One way of overcoming these limiting beliefs is to make growth a constant part of your life. It's normal to change weak beliefs. If you're not growing, you're dying. If you're not feeling that something new is coming along, then you are not evolving. You can enrich your life with empowering beliefs or by realizing that weak beliefs aren't supporting your dream. Your identity shapes your actions. Your identity has been formed from the past. You describe many parts of your identity as your belief system. You might say "I don't believe in politics, medicine or luck. I believe in every man for himself, taking care of my body naturally and through hard work." These beliefs form part of your self-image (identity) and ultimately affect how you behave and the decisions you make. Can you start to see that your identity is the nerve center or control tower of your actions? Now let's focus!

Remember I had you imagine that life is like a garden? By seeing the **eight plots in your Garden** as different parts of your personality, you can now focus more powerfully by putting your life into these categories:

- Emotions
- Spiritual
- Family & Friends
- Intimate Relationships

- Career
- Financial
- Hobbies
- Health

Emotions:	Spiritual:	Career:	Financial:
Family & Friends:	Intimate Relationships:	Hobbies:	Health:

Again, imagine each one has different sized trees and weeds. For example, if you didn't spend any time learning about your career, then you probably have lots of weeds in it. If you spend very little time learning about finances in the world we live in today, you will have a lot of weeds in that area of your garden too. In other words, financial stress. If you spend a lot of time on your relationship, then you're most likely going to have the fruits that reflect the care of nurturing that section of your garden or life. You will reap the benefits from giving it that attention and grow big, beautiful plump fruits that represent a joyous and happy relationship. You're responsible for the results that you get in your life. You may not totally believe that, but there's compelling evidence that says **everything you're getting in your life is a result of the choices that you have made.** We make hundreds of choices each day which dramatically affect our lives and shape our destiny.

The great news is that if you're not getting the results that you want, you can start to get them by modeling other people. By observing people who are getting the results that you desire and observing the trail of evidence that they leave behind —

the recipe or formulas that they're utilizing to harvest the crop of their choice — you too, can plant the same seed, adopt their system and get their results. You see, success is really simple. Just find someone using the formula then follow it in detail.

First We Make Our Habits And Then They Make Us!

Habits require that you respect certain principles, rituals or routines in your life. Habits, good or bad, can be hard to break. What we need to do is create the habits that are going to support us and give us the results that we want. I will show you how to create strong habits that are going to support you and how to destroy the habits that are holding you back. If you violate these principles or success rituals, you will experience pain.

The chains of habits are too weak to be felt until they are too strong to be broken.

— Samuel Johnson

I'm going to help you recognize the parts of your identity that limit you. Together we're going to replace them with the parts that will make you happy. Your identity is the father of your actions. All your actions emanate from the way you see yourself: your self-image. What we want to do is create a description of yourself so you will be compelled to take action to get the results that you want. Change requires the labor of learning to influence yourself through discipline, effort and methods of modeling. Because we're not taught these things in school, we often don't have the proper step-by-step method to undo the programming that we've been given. Your brain is basically an Information Processing Unit (IPU). If the information that has gone in has not been supporting you, then you need to change the input. You can't just get a different output, remember whatever goes in comes out, therefore garbage in/garbage out. You may have heard that you "reap what you sow." The bottom line is if you're saying to yourself, "I don't want to change, make more money or have more energy," yet deep down you really do, then you're not going to get the results you want. When we give energy to what we don't want and formulate this into words, we give it a negative life or vibration. As a result, the universe will be motivated to "match" that output or energy you're giving off. (The Law of Attraction.)

What you're lacking is a **method of modeling** and the ability to create exciting goals. What you are missing then is a strong belief that will support that outcome. For example, one of the beliefs that now supports me is *I can achieve anything I want if I'm committed and creative.* This statement can fuel one's potential even when the odds seem overwhelming.

Beliefs act like glasses through which you see, filtering or tainting the way you see everything. Imagine you go into a store that sells hundreds of sunglasses and you get to choose any pair that you like. The choices vary from: *I'm lazy, fat, tired, boring, a loser, stupid, mean, jealous, angry, I'm determined, a hard-worker, will give it my all, sexy, thoughtful, can achieve anything.* Most of these "sunglasses" have been given to you by your parents, teachers, religious leaders, friends and other role models. You try them on and soon they become a part of who you are and how you see yourself – whether they serve you or not! It colors how you see the world and when you believe it to be true it attracts the reality to you! Can you now imagine the person next to you who has a different set of sunglasses/beliefs who watches the very same thing you do, but that person sees opportunities rather than problems?

Belief controls our lives. It is one of the largest components of our identity. By learning to habitually change the glasses we wear, we shape our realities into the ones we consciously *choose,* instead of the ones we are unconsciously *living.*

By now, I hope you are getting excited. When I learned this, I certainly did! I could control and choose my beliefs (i.e. sunglasses) and transform the way I saw myself and my life, changing my results forever! If you don't feel compelled to change, it is generally for one of two reasons: a limiting belief or weak goals that are fueled by lack of desire. Your success is dependent upon your ability to consistently associate emotionally to your dreams and goals. I realized that from now on I would consciously choose my beliefs and make sure that they were empowering and not disempowering.

The problem isn't that most of us aim high and miss, it's that we aim low and hit. Then we get used to it and it becomes part of our negative identity, or how we see ourselves. **You are what you repeatedly do, said Socrates**, like shooting low, earning a lower income and having low energy. All of these things become part of your self-image. It's what you know which leads you to become familiar with it and finally addicted to it. It becomes a habit because we are all conditioned human beings. (Remember the elephant?) Through the exercises in this book, you will condition yourself to initialize the programming in the IPU of your mind. It is commonly believed by many that our minds are more powerful in storage capacity than all of the computers combined in the world today. It's time to tap in and experience the potential that lies within you because those dormant forces and faculties await your command.

Definiteness Of Passion

In life you do not get something for nothing. The laws of nature do not permit it, even though parts of us wish to get things for free. I do feel that you must give in order to receive. Yes, you must invest in yourself in order to reap the benefits of a constructed *you*; a *you* that you design by *choice* and not by *chance*. Not by random input through your circumstances with people who happen to be around you, but rather by fully constructing your goals and dreams. Having a definiteness in passion, a mission, vision and a purpose (MVP) that is in alignment with your nature ignites the real you — the *you* that you were meant to be.

What you must do is to stop investing in your fears and start embracing new emotions such as faith, courage and hope.

When you consistently do what you need to do whether you feel like it or not, you develop self-discipline and self esteem. Hold your MVP in your imagination and feed it daily, whether you are getting results or not. Pay the price of self-discipline and be a role model for those around you so that they can be inspired to support their dreams just as you do yours.

Ever notice that when you resist things, they keep on coming back to haunt you? Perhaps you resist exercise and then you are often sick. Or you resist doing your taxes on time and you have huge penalties and fall further in debt. You resist letting go of an employee only to find out that that person is costing the company a fortune.

Conversely, when you finally face things that appear scary they are rarely as bad as you think.

- When you exercise you feel better, have more energy and make better decisions.
- When you do your taxes on time, you save money, invest the savings, increase your wealth and lower your negative emotions of guilt and anxiety.
- When you let go of your under-producing employee and create a vacancy that gets filled by an unsuspecting junior employee, which adds value to your bottom line.

The truth has a way of taking all this weight off your mind. If you resist your reason for being here (your purpose) you will not be happy. If you resist being all that you can be, the universe will send challenges your way that will force you to grow and you will often be unprepared. Tension, pressure and "problems" all carry the seeds of growth, if you look for it rather than resisting the process. When we are in alignment with our deepest wishes, we are able to face our fears and set the appropriate standards for our lives. This way we are the ones who choose our battles and we arrive best prepared.

Otherwise, if we set the bar too low then life lifts it for us, making it unpredictable and usually more painful.

How To Motivate Yourself

You should never compare yourself to others. If you do, one of two things will happen: you'll have the JS or the JC syndrome. The JS is what I call the "Jerry Springer Syndrome." This means that at any point in your life you will always find somebody who is worse off than you: someone who appears less smart, less healthy, less spiritual, less fair, less kind, etc. You may feel better about yourself momentarily, then you will lose your drive by comparing yourself to these people. The JC, the "Jesus Christ Syndrome" is when you always find people who are better off than you. I use "Jesus Christ" as an example, assuming that we agree that Jesus Christ is as close to perfect as possible. We say, "Well I can never be like that. I don't have the resources; I don't have the knowledge; I don't have the beliefs, the values, the looks, height, education…" thus decreasing our drive.

You need to only compare yourself to your former self. Comparing to others will cause you to feel better or worse and neither serves you! This is effective only if you see them as a role model with the intent to model and learn from them in order to understand what is possible for you.

— **Rock Thomas**

I remember comparing myself to the cool kids at school and thinking, "I just can't compete with them. I don't belong in that gang or in that group. I can't chase the cute girls because I'm not as cool as so-and-so," only to find out later at my high school reunion that many girls inquired as to why I was so shy and bashful and didn't approach them. (Darn! What a missed opportunity!)

Growing up, I used to compare myself to my older brother and I felt discouraged. He was faster, funnier, smarter and stronger. During school, I would compare myself to the <u>most popular</u> kid in the classroom and feel lonely and sad. When I played hockey, I compared myself to the hardest working, <u>fastest</u> and best shooter – and I felt inferior to them all. When I was a sales person, I compared myself to the <u>top in my office</u>. When I was the best in my office, I compared myself to the best in the province. When I was the best in the region, I compared myself to the best in country. I always felt less than all of them. I never savored the joy of being the best *me* I could be at that time.

I remembered comparing myself to every speaker I ever listened to when I thought of beginning my speaking career. I thought I could never be as articulate as they were or as down to earth, dynamic, intelligent, organized or energetic. And every time I thought that, it made me feel like I was less than they were. This caused me to live in emotions of fear and anxiety, which is completely unnecessary. You will always find people who are better than you or people who appear to be geniuses in their given field. Surprisingly more often than not, we are unaware of how hard they've worked at obtaining the level of skill that they have. I've since learned that geniuses and those with high levels of achievement have paid the price of practicing in private (PPPP), yet we assume that it came to them easily. This often causes us to reduce our drive, thinking that they have talent that we don't. History has shown us that greatness is created through deliberate practice.

Sure, these people acted as motivators for me and spurred me on; however, the quality of my life was dependant on the emotions that I experienced while I was working toward my goals. There is a time to compare yourself to others as inspiration for what is possible and a time to realize that you are not them and they are not you. You may have focused on other parts of your garden (life) while they focused primarily on that one area. Take peoples' careers, for instance.

If the top salesperson is an older lady or gentlemen, then they have raised their kids and have years of contacts and experience. A younger salesperson compares himself to the top salesperson and discounts the fact that he is still raising his children while coaching soccer two nights a week. This causes the younger salesperson to have a feeling of disempowerment. Exclaiming that "I can never be like her" will not get you more of what you want, but will make you feel like there is little point in tapping into the best of you and persisting until you succeed. This form of comparison does no good. A better form of comparison would be to use them as a springboard to potentiality. Seeing them as your mentor/hero rather than a rival, will motivate and empower you. This type of comparison is OK. (For a more in-depth analysis, read my book *Inside the Power of Learning*.)

The fact of the matter is that you should compare yourself only to yourself. For example, compare the "you" of the future to the "you" of the past. See the "you" of the future as the perfect you, the best you, the optimal you, the brilliant you. It's "the you" that represents the characteristics and the traits that you wish to move toward creating – the best "you" possible. Compare where you are today with the person you desire to be and that will create your gap. Compare yourself only to yourself — the picture of you in the future. Your optimal self is your personal best without all the excuses. Make an "ideal" picture and say "Ok, I am over here and I want to get over there." Every day that you spend more time with the image that you desire to be more like (more patient, skillful, articulate, expressive, loving, joyful or caring), you will find yourself being pulled toward that behavior. You will feel better and better as you get closer to your "image." If you fall back, forgive yourself, get back on your horse and charge courageously forward.

Who Is Programming Your Identity?

Understand this: your identity is being formed daily. It has been forming over the years you have been alive into something that has good and bad traits – at least in your mind. This book will take you on the journey of eliminating the negatives and inserting a new programming of positives. This will revolutionize your life, your results and your levels of joy and fulfillment.

Back to my acne story: upon my return to Canada my acne was improved but I still had the self-image of a boy with acne. It was only recently that I have been able to accept the fact that this is not my self-image anymore (how I saw myself and felt others saw me). So powerful were those past images of myself, that I carried them with me even though the pimples were long gone.

Put-Downs Are Abundant

It has been estimated that kids have been put down over 100,000 times before they become adults. By the time they're 14 years old, 95% of our kids have a negative self-concept or identity. The way that they see themselves (or that they think that others see) is negative.

Is Our Family Helping Or Hurting?

Growing up with two brothers and three sisters I was often told to be quiet or laughed at because what I said did not make sense. We were somewhat like the Brady Bunch. My father remarried and I was the youngest in the family. My sister, foster brother and I joined my step-brother and his two sisters on their farm. We were from the city. It was an intimidating experience, to say the least. Often I was told that I had nothing of importance to say. I developed the self-image of an introverted, meek, skinny kid who hid from conversations when I so desperately wanted to be part of the fun and jokes. Because of the incessant feedback and ridicule from my brothers and sisters, I felt so much pain but I chose to say nothing again and again. I was molding my "identity." For almost all of us, our identities are being formed without our conscious consent. We need to be very careful because we see ourselves in terms of how others see us. Our need to have our behavior be consistent with how we describe ourselves is powerful. We are receiving feedback all the time when we are growing up. For instance, if you were chosen last to play sports, you might have retreated to seclusion during lunch times. If you were great at spelling, you might have tried out for the spelling team. These events shaped your identity without your necessarily knowing it. As you look into your memory bank, when you recall the activities that most likely gave you pleasure, you feel joy and confidence. The opposite is also true of painful memories.

Parents. Many parents unknowingly practice saying negative things to their children until those negatives become part of their child's identity. Their child internalizes these negatives, repeating them over and over to themselves. Parents can plant seeds of negativity in their children without even knowing it.

For example: Little Bobby is playing in the front yard while his mother and her friend are talking about the flowers. Suddenly Bobby sees something on the other side of the street, which attracts his eye. Three-year-old Bobby darts across just as a neighbor is backing out of the driveway. Mom shrieks, "Bobby!!!!!!!!!!!!! Stop!! Get back here!" Meanwhile, Bobby feels as if a bolt of lightening has gone through his body. All of a sudden he is not BEHAVING the right way anymore. He is wrong and has to change his behavior in order to be loved again by Mommy. This is the meaning he is likely to attach to the **tonality** he has never heard before.

Intellectually Bobby cannot handle it and *emotionally* it creates an **Extreme Emotional Experience™** (Triple E™) in his neurology. By yelling at him, his mother achieves her outcome on practical terms. She causes little Bobby to hesitate the next time he goes out onto the road. This is the beginning of feeling as though we have to please people in order to be loved. Our self-image starts to be shaped based upon the pain or pleasure we associate with events in our lives. The following other phrases are commonly used, yet are extremely harmful:

"Hurry up! You're always late!"

"You can't possibly be mine."

"You're an embarrassment."

"Why do I always have to run after you?"

"You never do what I ask."

"If you don't stop that, you can't have _____ / can't do _____."

"You're not smart like your sister."

"Why are you *so* slow?"

"You'll never amount to much."

"You're embarrassing me!"

"Quiet! I've had enough of your misbehaving."

"You were a mistake. A disgrace to this family."

"When will you learn? Probably, never?!"

"That's not good enough. Do it again."

"That is impossible!"

"Shut up, stop, no, careful, you'll get hurt, you know nothing, you'll learn the hard way, don't grow up like your father, who do you think you are anyway…wait until your father gets home… go to your room until you smarten up, sit down, hurry up, you're always… late, slow, forgetful, careless, hopeless, tired, angry, lazy, messy, you never remember anything, you just don't… care, understand, think…"

The list goes on and on.

When Bobby is a few years older, he becomes timid and afraid to make a mistake so he takes on a job that requires little risk. He slowly shrinks down into a life of despair.

The idea here is not to alarm you about going into the past. It is simply to say that what happens to you creates an effect. It's essentially the law of cause and effect. The result is called your identity.

The KEY here is to know that you can change your identity to whatever you want it to be. Understanding what has affected you will assist you in making the changes you desire.

Let us begin with the end in mind. Remember: in life we want one of two things:

1) To change a behavior

2) To feel a certain emotion

Your identity is made up of your beliefs, habits and values as well as your rules (things that you feel must happen in order for you to feel good or bad). Some examples of rules are:

- If she loves me, she will take care of me.
- As president, I must have that parking spot.
- If I make a million dollars, I am a success.
- If she says yes, then I will feel <u>loved</u>.
- If I get the promotion, then I will be a <u>success</u>.
- If I lose the game, I will be <u>upset</u>.
- If I beat so and so, I will be <u>happy</u>.
- If someone dies, I will mourn forever.

Feelings (love, success, overwhelmed, happiness) are the *end values*. Money, cars, sports, work and relationships are the *mean values*, the vehicles that help make us feel those end values we call feelings. What we ultimately are after. We all have **thousands of rules** that help us direct our emotional states.

Even if you say you want to be a millionaire, you actually want the feelings that you believe will come with becoming a millionaire, whether <u>respect</u>, <u>freedom</u> or <u>power</u> etc. So in order to create lasting change in your life, you must affect the CAUSE of your habits, beliefs, values and rules – not the symptoms. The actions that you take daily, good or bad, get deposited into your bank account of experience and we call them our memories. You have heard people say, "I would never go skydiving or bowling. That's just not me!" Yet a few years later you see them doing just what they said they would never do. What happened? Well they changed or expanded their identity and this allowed them to take a new action. Herein lies the key to change! But how did they do it and why?

You may recall that we are all motivated by the desire to have as much pleasure (or what we feel is pleasure) as possible and to avoid as much pain as possible. We tend to associate pain with different things and most of the time it has to do with our conditioning and with our education. Whenever an individual perceives that there is no choice in what they are about to do, the capacity to tap into their personal power increases when they feel it is an absolute must. For instance, in the armed forces people are pushed beyond what they feel they would ever do on their own. Another example would be when 9/11 occurred, people stepped outside of their identities to perform whatever it took to make a difference. This tells us that when people feel they have no choice, they step up and perform the improbable. The power to influence yourself depends greatly on your ability to manage what you attach pain and pleasure to, creating more "musts" than "maybes."

If you attach pain to exercising, you will do whatever you can to avoid this activity. This may manifest itself by your rationalizing, blaming or justifying as a way to explain your lack of action. The gym is too far, the membership costs too much, when the kids have less going on… You are the master of your destiny when you have developed the ability to link negative consequences through your imagination creating imaginary pain for a short burst. Then you will become a master at motivating yourself, rather than waiting for an outside force to determine your destiny.

Let's say you know you want to quit smoking, but you are unable to visualize the consequences. Months later you have a heart attack and now you are able to find the will-power to stop smoking immediately because the consequences become real. You had the capacity to quit before, but you didn't link enough consequences to quitting. You probably had softened the potential harm in your mind, saying "Oh, that won't happen to me" or "I'll quit after this pack." But when you had the heart attack, your body stopped and you knew the next step was death. Suddenly after the Triple E™ you had enough reasons to change your behavior. The consequences were more real and caused you to change your behavior. Now, picture if you had imagined the consequences of your smoking before. Couldn't you have stopped sooner? Of course you could have. Yet this muscle of using pain and pleasure as leverage is often highly under-used by those getting average results. You are your past, in that you are the perception of your past. How you have replayed your experiences to yourself and how you have interpreted them will lead you to who you think you are. We give ourselves titles and labels based upon our perceptions of the past. You see yourself as a reflection of those labels and from the feedback that you have received from others. Perhaps you see yourself as being funny, smart or kind, based largely on how people have reacted to your behavior. You may not think of yourself as a result, but you most certainly are. Many people have influenced our youthfully pure minds while we were growing up. Not all were of good intent, and those who thought they were may not have known about the laws of success. Being of good intentions is not enough.

I will give you an example. Suppose you are growing up and your grandparents play a major role in your upbringing. They lost one of their children in a car accident and another one of their kids was badly injured in a motorcycle accident. They have massive fear associated with losing anyone that is close to them. And there you are, four years old and you are about to go on your bike on the street, a quiet cul-de-sac:

"Grandma I am going bike riding!" you exclaim proudly. "Do you want to watch?"

"Oh, my pet," she says "Are you sure you want to go? It is very dangerous. Why don't you stay in here and we can watch TV together?"

While Grandma equates watching TV to being safe and pain-free, you are a child and do not know differently. How you respond to this will shape your identity. You spend every afternoon with your grandparents and they (meaning well, of course) overwhelm you with these statements every time you visit. As a child, you are naturally playful so out you go on the bike and Grandma comes to make sure nothing goes wrong. She is calling out things like, "Be careful! Not too fast! Watch out – there is a car coming! Don't fall!" At times when you are a little wobbly and she screams projecting her fear, you become more uncertain, thinking that it must be really bad if you fall. Of course, what you focus on tends to happen. You think, "I better not fall, I better not fall," and then Grandma yells out and you go down. She runs over to you and says, "Didn't I tell you, you would fall? Didn't I tell you that you were going to hurt yourself?" You think Grandma knows best, so you feel you should listen to her. You become fearful of future events when Grandma says "Be careful" again muting your behavior and identity, causing you to take less and less risks even though most are not life-threatening! Eventually Grandma's fears become programmed into your brain and you become less than you could be. After some time the TV looks more and more attractive and less painful. Soon your identity is negatively shaped by someone who is well-meaning and loving. Dozens of these events (Triple E™) take place by accident, but they shape your mind and your identity.

I grew up on a farm. We had parents who did not believe in babying their children. My father went through WWII and he believed that the world was a tough place and it was his job to prepare me for that place. One day I was kicked in my arm by a pony and went crying to him. He said to me that it looked as though it was bruised and to stay away from the ponies for a little while; it would heal itself. I was 10 years old at the time and it was my job to feed 20 horses each morning. I carried on even though I felt extreme pain because I did not want to let my dad down and be a whiner. The next weekend I went to visit my mom (my parents were divorced) and complained of pain in my arm. She took me to the clinic and discovered that my arm had been broken. Because it had started to heal incorrectly, it had to be broken again and then put in a cast. Upon my arrival back at my dad's that Sunday night, my father told me that I was overreacting and that my mother would turn me into a sissy. Another Triple E™.

To this day I have been able to put up with high levels of pain and tolerate extremely harsh working environments. Whether it is long hours or double shifts, I have been able to tolerate it because this has become part of my identity. I attached the meaning of being a sissy and losing my father's respect (which meant pain to me), because I so wanted him to be proud of me. So I developed an identity of a strong, tough boy. I am not saying that my values are the right ones, but that this was how they were formed. *Nothing has meaning but the meaning we give to it.* Our past dictates how we interpret current events. You can keep the ones that serve you and support you, and you can change those that are negative and hold you back – if you have the burning desire to make the shift.

Nothing Has Meaning
But The Meaning You Attach To It

Some people love to exercise while many others do not. One person will actually love the feelings it gives them while the other will attach pain to the activity and do almost anything to avoid it. Why you ask? Let me explain.

John loves to work out. He was not big growing up and he wanted to be more buff for the girls. He saw good looking guys getting the pretty girls so he attached massive pleasure (or at least potential pleasure) to being in shape because this gave him the best chance of getting a great looking girl, at least in his perception of the world.

John's father died of colon cancer. He had been told several times that he should exercise, yet his father kept on putting it off. He put it off for so long that it became part of his identity, making it harder for him to get himself to take action even if he intellectually knew that it was the right thing to do.

John observed his father's death from cancer and linked the fact that his father did not exercise as one of the contributing factors. Armed with the knowledge that exercise reduces the chances of cancer, John thought "I don't want to die young like my dad. I'd better exercise." You see, the pain was attached to not exercising rather than to exercising. Furthermore, he used *both* of the Twin Towers of Motivation (Pleasure and Pain). The potential pleasure was being healthy and attractive to women, so John attached the meaning of pleasure to working out, while attaching high levels of pain to not exercising. His future behavior is predictable and is now part of his identity.

Your identity is like a recipe for a great cake. You cannot make the cake if the key ingredients are missing. You will struggle to take action if the ingredients do not show up in your personality description or your identity. What I mean is that if you were to look inside at the way that you see yourself you would have a picture of yourself and a description saying that you are: adventurous, outgoing, successful, 20 lbs overweight, lazy, selfish, smart, clever, witty, casual dresser, etc. Now if you desire to bake a cake of a public speaker or tennis player, you look inside and check your ingredients. If there are none that say public speaker, tennis player or whatever it is that you are being requested to perform at that time, your mind will say: "Sorry we do not have that skill available. Just say no thanks. I AM NOT A TENNIS PLAYER OR A PUBLIC SPEAKER."

You may think, "If I am adventurous, then I would try it." Perhaps your mind will say, "Ok let's have fun" and your conscious mind asks "OK, what does that mean?" Well, we will give it our best even if we do not have a lot of references. It may be embarrassing, so be ready to laugh at yourself. Unfortunately many of us lose our adventurous side over time! And those who don't are often looked at with envy as they have the young spirit alive and well within them.

Will your performance be affected by this internal verification of your identity? You bet it will. This is happening all the time for everything you do. How you approach things in your life and how you rate them (pain or pleasure) will determine your decisions and your direction and ultimately your entire life. Yet, most of us are adopting our beliefs and values randomly. It is time to stop this! After today, you should begin to realize how and when this is happening to prevent the continual construction of a haphazard identity. Shaping your identity and consciously choosing what it is that you are going to move toward and become is a choice. If you commit to do so, it will transform your life beyond your wildest dreams.

This information will open the door to personal happiness, success and wealth. I have studied the most successful people in the world. By successful, I mean people who are getting the results that THEY desire and that makes them feel fulfilled. In other words, living life on their terms. Isn't that the key? To be able to live life on your terms! To get the results that you want on a consistent basis. THAT is what I am going to show you, a simple process to results — daily.

Changing Your Self-Image

At this stage, you should be able to accept that your self-image can be changed. Did you have incidents that caused you to believe things that made you feel weak or unable to achieve your inner desires and dreams? Look at the heroes before you — they too, were exposed to circumstances that gave them the chance to develop a poor or weak identity. Yet they still discovered the way to empowerment and created their optimal self. Virtually all heroes have overcome the odds of their circumstances and have learned how to change the meaning of what has happened to them from weak to strong. As you are faced with your biggest challenges in life, you are given the greatest chance to transform your identity. Yet, most miss the opportunity — they lack the strategy.

Those who are faced with overwhelming circumstances often come to realize that they have untapped potentials (reserves) that were dormant. It's the discomfort or dissatisfaction with their current situation that motivates them to tap into those dormant energies and activate them. When we are faced with a crisis, life demands that we step up. Many people have proven that some things really are not that impossible — from Oprah Winfrey to Lance Armstrong, from miracle recoveries to modern science —we are breaking new ground everyday. All is possible when mental gymnastics are coupled with a proper mental diet. You have all the potential in the world. It has been said that most of us do not access more than about 10% of our brain's potential power. Your ability to process everything that is going on around you is virtually limitless for the unconscious mind. Accessing that data and bringing it to the conscious mind is where we have more of a challenge. Scientists have taken scans of the brain and recognize that there is no difference in the areas of the brain that become activated from when one is experiencing the event to imagining the event. Furthermore, doctors performing brain surgery have witnessed the total recall of childhood events down to the last detail when certain areas of the cortex are stimulated. It is a commonly held belief that **we have perfect memories yet struggle to recall these events**, leading us to feel that we are not intelligent. Hypnosis would further support these findings. When individuals are put under hypnosis they have been able to recall events again down to the smallest of details while consciously they are able to only recall a fraction of the same information.

Scientific data proves that we have potential for genius. You are truly a genius. It is important that you believe it. That you really have this ability to do so much more than you are currently doing or achieving. Whether you decide to act upon that has nothing to do with your potential but rather with your ability to motivate yourself. Look at *Ripley's Believe It or Not* and you will see that people are pulling trucks with ears and piercing their bodies with objects. That just does not make sense. Yet, they believe it and it comes to pass. We must recognize that we are limitless – with the exception of those limits that we impose on ourselves and those that were imposed on us while we were unaware that we had a choice to accept or refuse them. Today, you have a choice to **believe** that which will empower you or to believe that you cannot change and that you are stuck. Because you are reading this book, I believe you realize deep down that you can change.

When I coach people I often ask them, "Who are you?" Many people I have heard say "Well, I don't know who I am!" Or they will give a half-hearted attempt to say what they think I want to hear. Even if you think you don't know who you really are, you do know! You have to push past your reflexive answer of saying you don't. When you go shopping and the salesperson approaches you and asks "May I help you," do you realize that 99% of us, even if we really want some help, will have the reflexive reply of "No thanks, I'm only looking"? So in fact, you know who you are at the "core," but you have been pleasing so many others for so long that you may have lost sight of what you really are. You have become conditioned in a pattern that has been working for you, yet it is not leading you to fulfillment. So has it really been working for you? Now is the time to find out.

Your Garden Of Life

Please look at the garden of your life and take a moment to notice that your life has been divided (chunked) into eight areas. The reason for this is that you will have more clarity if you are able to focus or concentrate on one area of your life at a time. Past history shows that most of us have great results in one area yet we are failing miserably in others. This puts us out of balance and creates stress. If our goal is to avoid pain and to gain pleasure and we are stressed at a core level, then to get out of it we need to build ourselves up from the root, not from the fruit. Treating the fruit or the external part of us will not work. We need to treat the root. This is an inside job. For each area you have on some level a description of your identity, a way that you see yourself and therefore how you behave accordingly. To a large degree it is also how you think others expect you to be.

Exercise

Describe who you are today. To assist you with discovering who you are, ask yourself these questions:

- Who am I?
- How do others see me or describe me to be?
- What have I been doing mostly in each area of my garden?
- What have I contributed, shared?
- Am I happy, easygoing, friendly, wealthy, healthy, energetic, athletic, strong, determined, romantic, entrepreneur, loving, motherly?
- Am I short-tempered, cranky, easily agitated, pompous, egotistical, condescending, greedy, selfish, jealous, lonely, fearful, timid, weak, tired, hateful, revengeful, stupid, lazy, procrastinating?

Complete the eight plots and write in who you have been up to today. Not how you would like to be, but how you have been living your life up to the present. Pick up your pen and fill in the square. Thinking of how someone else would describe you can help as well.

Example:

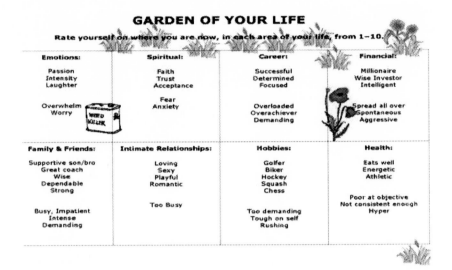

Ok, now fill in your key words to describe who you have been.

Emotions	Spiritual
□	□

<u>Family & Friends</u>   <u>Intimate Relationships</u>

Career	Financial
□	□

<u>Health</u>	**<u>Hobbies</u>**
☐	☐

Gifts, Talents and Strengths

ACTION: *Highlight the traits you wish to keep and become appreciative of.*

When this is completed, you will be able to extract the character traits that are <u>positive</u> and that have served you to your success. Evolution is based on capturing and keeping the best of what works, while discarding the negative.

Notice that there is something positive that has allowed you to get results in some (or every) area(s) of your life. Can you carry that forward to other areas, and bring strength into those areas as well?

Negative Traits

ACTION: *Cross out the negative traits.*

Perhaps you've indulged in self-pity, laziness or procrastination. Have you been lonely and fearful, taken a back seat or been timid? Have you believed others when they said that you were too young or too old, ugly or overweight? Have you been possessive and judgmental or perhaps jealous and critical? These are the areas of improvement that you can target if you desire to upgrade and or expand your self-image. For now just become aware of what they are and that they have not been working for you. These traits are not you they are how you have been behaving and you can change that by changing the way you see yourself.

Reach For Clarity

ACTION: *Enter your number from 1 to 10 in the box provided.*

- Now give yourself a number for each section of your garden based on a scale of one to 10, where one is desperately depressed and 10 is phenomenally happy and fruitful. Don't forget to note the date.
- Once this is completed, sit back and access where you

are in your life.
- What are you passionate about?
- Where do you desire improvement?
- How are you going to make that happen?
- Which garden plot needs the most attention right now?
- Which one has received the most attention in the past?
- Which elements or characteristics are missing for you to achieve your life's purpose?
- If you were more _____ would you be the kind of person who would achieve the results you wish to receive? Keep in mind that you desire certain emotions — happiness, respect, love, excitement, joy — which are end values, yet most of us focus on means values in an attempt to get there without clearly knowing our options. (Example: Buying a car might make us feel important and respected for a while. Yet being self-disciplined and doing what needs to be done whether we feel like it or not can give us lasting feelings of importance and respect that cannot be taken away. Can you see the difference?)

Summary

Here's what you have accomplished so far:

- Your old identity is written out and you have clarity.
- You've highlighted the traits you feel good about and would like to keep because they serve your MVP (your Mission, Vision and Purpose).
- You've crossed out your negative or disempowering traits (often brought on by those Triple E™ experiences from your past) so that you can focus on ripping those weeds out of your garden and maintaining a healthy and robust garden (identity).
- You understand the use of Pain and Pleasure to motivate yourself and you will practice being aware of the consequences of **not doing** what needs to be

done! Likewise, you will equate pleasure with **doing** the things you know you should, by focusing on the benefit of doing them rather than the pain of doing them.

- You are excited now because the awareness of how you have been shaped combined with the tools to change are now within your grasp!

Let's now focus for a bit on your MVP and then we will complete your **ultimate identity** through your Mission, Vision and Purpose.

Chapter 2:

Inside The Power Of Your Purpose

Success is not the result of spontaneous combustion. You must set yourself on fire.

— **Reggie Leach**

Before determining your optimal self, we need to dig down and find out what we are passionate about. Then things will grow in our garden. In fact, they will flourish.

High performance comes from high purpose. Most of us want to make a difference, to contribute, to create a lasting meaning in our everyday tasks. If you know **your purpose** and the legacy that you want to be remembered for, you will have the drive to get you past any obstacle. Once you've found your purpose, the one that excites you and adds value to others' lives, you will never worry about your finances again. **The only people among us who will truly be happy are those who have sought and found a way to serve others.** When it is no longer about the money and it is truly about serving, the abundance comes. I call this knowing your MVP! Your Mission, your Vision, your Purpose.

Discover Your MVP

Let's clearly define your MVP.

Mission: Your day-to-day stepping stones, which help you to arrive at your vision and gives a worthy meaning to each task (even the most mundane) as they form the pieces to your purpose and the reality of your vision.

Vision: The process of imagining what it looks, feels and tastes like. Using your senses to describe and depict what you want in your mind so that you have clarity about the path that needs to be taken to get you to the result you want. The ability to visualize the end result in any area of your garden.

Purpose: Your *why*. The reasons that compel you to keep on going, regardless of the challenges along the way.

So how do you discover your MVP? Take a few minutes each day and answer the following questions:

- What do I want?
- What do I truly want?
- What is the **purpose** of my life?
- What do I want to be remembered for?
- How do I want others to refer to me?
- What's my legacy? What do I want to leave behind?
- Who do I want to affect? Who do I want to be a role model for?

Run through those questions. Answer any of them at random. Do this consistently. Do this every day. Continue to demand from your mind, the answer for every question — it must produce an answer. Meditate, dwell, invest time focusing on these questions and the answers they bring. If your mind initially says, "I don't know," push for another answer. Do not accept the reflex answer, "I don't know." **That's just old conditioning.** It's just what you've become accustomed to saying to yourself. We're going to rip apart what you know and expand it until you get to the truth and start to feel the joy of pure purpose every day. *Discovering Your Purpose* is about going below the surface of your garden and planting new seeds (new information) and focusing on things that are important to you. This means thinking, talking and telling others about your dreams and your vision for your purpose.

It Starts By Feeding The Seeds Of Your Dreams

At times even the people who love you will try to talk you out of your dreams in the hopes of protecting you. People who have given up on their dream will try to shoot yours down. This can happen to you every day. That's why you need enough fuel to energize it. You need to give it life, have it set you on fire and light up your soul. Fear will show up — it's natural. But don't let it stop you. Persist beyond with faith in your mission.

I truly believe that each and every one of us is put here for a purpose. You are unique and special. Allow yourself to feel that and honor yourself for being special. Creating the identity of a successful inner mindset will allow you to progress every day.

All of our lives we've been taught to get an education and a good job, which means helping somebody else live their dream. That's great, but our education doesn't stop there. If you're not getting the results that you want in your life, if you're not completely fulfilled, there is a very good chance that you don't have an overall purpose. Commit to investing some time to do that. If you want fulfillment and happiness, it's not about trying to avoid the decisions of life and staying stuck in what you already know. I promise you, that will not make you happy. You will get bored and will eventually lead yourself to distractions like overeating, TV, drinking, drugs, etc., in order to change the way you feel because you're not experiencing the growth that you want in your life. What you need is an overall compelling future (your purpose) – a reason for you to get up in the morning and create something new, to add value, to make a difference, to contribute to society, to contribute to your own life and well-being. To be a role model and leave behind a legacy, you must have something that lives on beyond you.

The fastest way that you create change in your life is to become passionate and enthusiastic about it. Nothing great was ever achieved with a little bit of interest — get passionate about your purpose. Creating a purpose for your life is done through the process you read about in the opening section. **Ask questions regularly and your purpose will appear.**

Once you feel you have an overall MVP for your life, bring it down to one simple phrase: "The MVP of my life is to..." and make sure that <u>it is</u> obtainable daily.

Example: The purpose of my life is to be my personal best in everything I do, while enjoying the moment and being positive for those around me.

Once you have clarity of purpose, the lack of resources will be one of your challenges. Understanding who and what will try and stop you is crucial to your success. Whether it be the lack of time or money or knowledge – these obstacles become the hurdles with which you will shape your character; therefore, it is worth mentioning that being grateful for our obstacles is the approach reserved for the enlightened. Of course I encourage this of you.

What Is The Purpose Of An Obstacle?

Think about your favorite sports team. Or, if you're an athlete yourself, what is it like to play somebody who you know is much weaker than you and you know you can easily beat? Do you get excited about that game? Do you bring the best of yourself to that game? Does your favorite team have to play their best and put their key players in the situation and demand the best of them? No. They're not up against a worthy opponent. I would like to suggest an empowering belief: **obstacles are there as worthy opponents.** When you are equipped with a powerful MVP, a powerful identity (self-image) and peak performance strategies (strategies, principles) you will inevitably succeed. How different would your life be if you relished your obstacles? You want to be able to know that heading into the game of life; you have a chance at winning. Not that you're guaranteed to win, because that certainty would be boring. You want the opportunity to sculpt yourself and to stimulate growth.

Example: Guy Leach is a six-time World Iron Man. When I interviewed him and I asked "What made you so successful?" He said, "The thought of my worthy opponents made me practice hard in preparation for the competition ahead." They drove him to be his best and pushed him beyond what he would do if he were not up against them.

Why We Don't Want To Have Problems

Problems are difficult, otherwise we wouldn't call them problems. They force us to go from what we know to what we don't know. The element of discomfort comes from not embracing the fact that we are given these problems to learn and grow. We want to be happy, to have fun, to expend less effort, have certainty and to feel no pain or suffering. Preferably we would not have to work either! Overcoming problems or obstacles, however, carries with it the opportunity for the greatest joy. Life will not give you happiness without your giving life your best. Yet most people try to cut corners and do less. He who solves the most problems is rewarded by life. Failures try to avoid their problems or work around them. Successful people embrace them, looking for the gift, the seed of opportunity that is hidden within. Working through these opportunities, even when we don't feel like it and we are experiencing some suffering gives life meaning.

Life is a series of problems. Do we want to moan about them or solve them?

— **M. Scott Peck**

We can hope and wish for no problems, complain and moan about our problems or accept life's challenges and work through them. The fact of the matter is life will not devote itself to making you happy. Once you are engaged in the philosophy of meeting challenges head-on you will find the tools to empower you. The universe will conspire to provide you with the necessary resources. Life is difficult only when we try to avoid our problems. It was not meant to be effortless — how could you grow if it was easy? People try daily to avoid their hardships, investing their energy in resisting rather than dealing with it. They talk as if their problems are unique and unsolvable, often talking to people who cannot and will not make a difference or help them solve their problems. What you focus on grows. Talking about your problems won't make them disappear, it makes them bigger. Remember, be thankful and focus on the solution. By accepting that things will require energy or will require some effort, we begin to focus on how to make it what we want it to be, rather than complaining about why it isn't that way.

Ask a great question. Look back on your past successes and ask, how did I handle them? This is a great place to start. By accessing our resources such as an empowering belief ("I can achieve anything I want, if I'm committed and creative") or a specific emotion: confidence, faith or courage. When attempting to find the resources we feel we lack, we can borrow the resources of somebody who has achieved that result before. This is known as modeling or acting "as if."

Example: You want open up a successful new business. You're not sure how to go about it. All you need to do is to use the power of modeling — look at people who have opened up those businesses before, then find out what their inner mindset and daily routines are made up of. Look at successful people with empowering beliefs and principles (like the ones outlined in this book) who have the ability to create confidence through courage, faith and creativity. Then do what they do, think like they think, and say what they say.

The number one reason that people do not model others is fear of failure. If they admit to their vision, goal, what they want and go after it, but don't achieve it, they will risk being labeled a failure. One of the biggest fears we all have as humans is the <u>fear of failure</u>. Yet, it's the truth that sets us free! There is one way to overcome your fear and that's to face it. Period! Fear is experienced on all levels. The higher you move up the ladder of success, the more you have to lose if you mess up. Fear doesn't disappear until you engage yourself into action. Action carries with it the antidote for fear. **Do what you fear and it will disappear. Avoid it and it will haunt you forever!** What you lack are simply the strategies or tools to get yourself to act in spite of your fears.

The Law Of Attraction

Your **RAS (Reticular Activating System)** makes you aware of things that are important to you, so why not use it to your advantage? All you need to do is put in your order in the form of your MVP. Then chunk those down into goals. Goals are just dreams in bite-size form with a deadline and a direction

Example: Imagine you're spending the night at a hotel. Your room is right next to the elevator shaft. You can hear the elevator from your bed while you try to sleep. Within a short period of time your RAS starts monitoring the ascents and descents of the elevator. Notice as time passes that your mind recognizes that it's not important to you, and therefore deletes it, thus blocking out the sound so you can go back to sleep. Shortly thereafter, you hear your baby cry. You are suddenly wide awake. It's because your unconscious mind knows your baby's cry is important. It knew what to look for on your behalf because you gave it instructions. If everyone understood the concept of letting yourself know what's important to you and the power of your RAS, I'm convinced that everyone would set goals and allow their unconscious minds to serve them.

Reticular Activating System

By focusing on what you want, thinking often and regularly about what you want, you activate your RAS. I encourage you to set goals in writing and then to start talking and thinking about them. Visualize them coming true. You will activate your RAS and the universe will conspire with you to help you achieve your dreams.

Example: I was looking for an assistant for one of my companies. I just said to myself, "Within the next week I'm going to find somebody who is going to be perfect for the position." I happened to be at a networking meeting. I was not focusing consciously when I was discussing some different business ventures and mentioned that I was expanding my business and looking for an assistant. This person happened to already be running a company, yet took a liking to my vision and felt my passion. Shortly afterward, she applied for the position. Learn to think, talk, and share your dreams and goals with others and the resources will follow.

Example: I was in the process of building one of my businesses and I noticed that there was somebody within my company who looked very sharp. I was looking for somebody who was strong in marketing. I had written down a goal stating that I wanted to enhance the marketing of one of my companies. One of the individuals was a real estate agent in my company and I noticed that every time we were involved in any kind of training, he was always bringing his laptop and adding value by putting together little charts and graphs and offering this as free information. My RAS went to work again. I pulled him in for an interview. Within a short period of time, this person started working for me in that department and has since achieved great success.

If I hadn't written down that I wanted to improve my marketing department, I believe that I would not have noticed his strength in that area and I might have overlooked him as a resource. My RAS might not have brought it to my attention, because I wouldn't have made it important. I hope these are good examples of how putting what you want to the forefront of your mind (by writing it down) and making it one of your desired outcomes will make your RAS work for you.

Life Isn't Fair — Get Over It

Looking at problems as unfriendly, unwanted events adds a negative mindset to a positive opportunity. In the section on Questions, we talk about asking yourself "What's great about this?"

Like taking a morning shower, make the planting of positive thoughts a daily practice.

— Neil Eskelin

61

I don't claim to be able to explain why all things happen, including unfortunate things to good people. Let's just say that we all have a path in life, a destiny or choice of what we create or manifest. Some say we hold a vibration and attract the equivalent back to us. Either way, once it happens, all you can control is your response. So why not develop the ability to embrace the challenges in your life?

Your life is the emotions that you live in. Decide to address your problems with an emotion that will allow you to be happiest. Pain is everywhere, but suffering is optional. People tend to learn more from pain than from pleasure. A fool will repeat his mistakes, while a wise person learns from them by deciding to look for the lesson. Fools, in a bizarre way, seem to lower their standards, thus increasing their tolerance for pain. It is not that successful people escape pain, they simply manage their choice of emotions wisely by seeing the good in each situation until it becomes a habit and part of their identity. You either win or learn! Losing is no longer an option!

Most of us are shaped by our environments. The few wise and successful people (about 3%) shape their character and identity by adding a powerful meaning to the events and "problems" in their lives. Those who don't are at the mercy of circumstance. They feel great when things are going great. When their team is winning, they feel great. When they get the raise that they want, they feel great. However, when things go bad they fall apart. Indeed, a fearful way to live.

Find the gift, the learning and decide to face each challenge and problem head-on with courage, faith and creativity until you develop such certainty that nothing intimidates you. Now that's freedom! It's knowing that regardless of what happens, you can live in the emotions of your choice, not in reaction but in creation. Say yes to life and all of its gifts. Many gifts are disguised as problems, challenges and hardships. Find the positive uplifting meaning that you will attribute to life's events and to yourself.

Your trek to the peak will have steep accents, slippery slopes and daunting moments. Say yes to it all! Practice makes permanent. So, learn to spend time developing your courage, creativity and faith.

Courage

Taking action in spite of your fear.

Creativity

Trying something new with the belief that you'll learn, grow and have joy. Looking for another way takes practice, trial and error.

Faith

Visualizing what has not been created, equipped with the belief that you'll find the way. Walt Disney, Thomas Edison and John F. Kennedy certainly did.

Your success will be dependent upon your ability to develop strong beliefs by attaching positive meanings to what happens in your life.

What Keeps You Going
When You Feel Like Quitting?

If you find a path with no obstacles, it probably doesn't lead anywhere.

— Frank A. Clark

Reasons! Your reasons are the essence of purpose, the purpose behind the plan. Having a purpose is even greater than the plan. While the two go hand-in-hand, the purpose is the fuel, not the mechanics. Most people focus on the plan. Then, when the plan gets a little bit tough to execute, they give up. The key is to have both, locked and loaded. We're not talking about the plan right now; we're talking about building the foundation, filling the rocket with fuel so that even after it reaches its destination, it still has reserves. If you're driving across the desert for 200 miles, you're not going to fill your gas tank up to cover 100 miles because you know you won't make it. You need gas for closer to 500 miles in the event of the unexpected. When you're going for something in your life that you want, you need more than enough fuel. You need a reserve tank in case you hit some stormy weather or some unknown obstacle that you didn't quite anticipate. It's a matter of planning for the worst, but expecting the best. And having plenty of desire/passion to spare. When you're passionate about it, you'll see that you will have no problem overcoming any worthy opponent.

Passion vs. Security

I once heard about a study done with 1,500 people: 83% of them have pursued a career based primarily on financial gain while 17% pursued their passion/what they loved to do. Out of the 1,500 people, 20 years later, there were 101 millionaires. Of the 101 millionaires, try to imagine which portion came from the 83% who followed the dollar sign. Zero. All of those who pursued their passion and did what made them happy became millionaires. Doing what you love is like not going to work. Therefore, you end up doing it well. There is so much value in doing what you love. The aliveness that you feel will be incredible.

Your obstacles will shrink as you keep your eye on the goal. Likewise, your obstacles will grow when you take your eye off of the goal. What you focus on grows and you get more of. It is crucial that you keep plenty of fuel by emotionally investing and thinking about your MVP. The lack of reasons (your fuel) will lead to failure or at best a date with mediocrity. Investing emotionally in the benefits will help you when the going gets tough. Associate to what you want as often as possible.

If You're Not Growing, You're Dying

The gift of an obstacle is the opportunity for you to grow. Again, watch how there is an underlying belief here. I believe that **if you're not growing, you're dying**. And, if you're not growing, you're not experiencing what's outside of your comfort zone and getting the juice of life. The gift is in knowing that you're going to go outside of your comfort zone (what you know) to a little bit of uncertainty. In that process, you are going to become more, thus expanding your identity. Just like my daughter who jumped off the diving board and felt excited about it. Because she did it again and again, she got to the point where that became her new comfort zone. But the gift for her, when she first did it, was expanding her comfort zone, expanding her identity and feeling juiced and jazzed about facing her fear.

> *What you love is a sign from your higher self of what you are to do.*
> — **Sanaya Roman**

You must really resonate well with your MVP — just discover what you love to do. Ask yourself "What would I do if I knew I could not fail?" Think about what you really love. Allow yourself to bathe in it. For a moment, remove the fear. Think of the acronym FEAR as False Evidence Appearing Real. Just remove that for a while. Let it go. What would you do if you knew you could not fail?

> *Problem with the rat race is that even if you win, you're still a rat.*
> — **Lily Tomlin**

Unfortunately, many of us get caught in the rat race and before we know it we're addicted to the material world. We move away from where we are and detract ourselves by becoming involved in the material world. Remember, in school they don't teach us how to manage our finances or our emotions. This book is about your inner mindset. Learning to perform at your peak is going to allow you to manage your mind, emotions and your feelings of fear, which ultimately will hold you back from being successful financially. Find out what it is that you love. Follow the processes in this chapter and discover what your purpose truly is. You will find yourself being compelled to achieve outstanding results.

Uncertainty and mystery are energies of life. Don't let them scare you unduly, for they keep boredom at bay and spark creativity.
— **R.I. Fitzhenry**

Creating Your Purpose: Planting The Seeds

God, grant me the serenity to accept the things I cannot change, the courage to change the things I can, and the wisdom to know the difference.
— **Dr. Reinhold Niebuhr**

Don't allow your dreams to be limited by what others say or do. It comes from within you, what you think about most and create with your imagination. This is often the catalyst for what you dream. You can also use your hatred as a motivator to create massive energy. For example, Mothers' Against Drunk Driving, Lance Armstrong, Mother Theresa and Oprah were all propelled by their hatred for something, a pain that was created in them. Conversely, rationalization, justification, apathy, fear, worry, as well as friends and siblings with low standards are dream busters. These are all the people who will keep you distracted from discovering what your dream is and keep you from using your creative imagination to tap into your MVP.

Inside the Power of Visualization

The first question you need to answer will be "How do I want to finish the game of life?" You can look at many of the great writers of our time, Stephen Covey being one of them. He talks about "beginning with the end in mind." Others say, don't start until you've finished. Really, what it means is for you to go into your mind's eye (into the creative part of your mind) and to look at the finished product. Look at what you want for your life, whether you are a sculptor, a painter, a carpenter, an architect or a lawyer — nothing begins until you first imagine it clearly in your mind. See the end product or result.

You must have a picture of tomorrow. Most people feel inadequate or inferior. The antidote is faith in your creativeness. Believe that you can draw unlimited abundance from the universe to fulfill your desires. A well-fed dream is a picture of the vision of what is first imagined in your mind and then created by you in your environment. What qualifies as your total focus equals your dream, with or without the support of others. Whether it is the passion of young men in the movies *The Karate Kid* or *Rudy* or something that Rosa Parks did — they all required a predominant obsession about their futures.

What dominates your thoughts and your conversations do so because they are more than likely linked to your dreams. You will not be able to not talk about them. You will be activated when somebody else is talking about something that has to do with your MVP, your dream. What happens in your mind will most often happen in your future. Visualization will create increase. Talk will create increase. Each day will move you toward connecting you to your dream. Those who dare to dream, plant and visualize their dream with emotionalized energy will see it materialize. Plant the seeds to reap the rewards of all your dreams. All things are created twice: first in your mind and then in your life. Understand when you invest in "that which is right," wrong people will find you unbearable. Plant your dream. Plant the seeds in the garden of your mind. Successful people think about what they want until they achieve it. Every dream will come with its enemies (weeds). Expect it, prepare for it and overcome it.

Once you have found a way to consistently bring value to the marketplace, you will earn the opportunity to give life to your dream. You will be remembered for your ability to focus. Your dream serves to make you focus. All failure can be traced back to broken focus. Your dream will serve as a guide for you. Dreams follow massive preparation. Practice makes perfect, practice makes permanent. How you perform on the stage of life is based on how you invest your thoughts and practice in preparation for that performance. Declare your dreams and this will attract others with similar dreams, values and beliefs. Your dreams will attract others who have met theirs. Many have their dreams dashed on the rocks of temporary defeat. Seeing your success, their hopes will become alive.

Light The Fire Of Your Burning Desire

You may have heard the story about a young boy who seeks out Socrates to ask him, "Socrates, what is the purpose of my life?"

Socrates offers, "It's not for me to decide, but it is for you to decide."

The boy says, "I don't know what to do."

Socrates says, "Come with me." He leads him down to the river and takes him into the river up to his waist. He forces the young boy's head under the water and holds it down with his two hands. The young boy tries to get up. Socrates holds his head down as he fights to get up. Socrates pushes harder down. The fight continues. Socrates pushes his head down again until finally the boy breaks free and comes up gasping for air.

Panting for air, the boy shrieks out, "What are you doing?"

Socrates said, "The moment that you desire something with the same passion and intensity that you desired for oxygen – that is the moment you will be connected to your purpose and passion." You must want it so badly that you can taste it, fight for it. To be willing to do whatever it takes in order to make it come to pass. It is only when you hunger for something that badly, that you will know that you are connected to your purpose.

How Do You Want To Be Remembered?

Ask yourself: How do I want to be remembered? What will be my legacy? As you ask those questions again and again, you will find your purpose will start to surface. As you feel it write it out. Having clarity about your purpose may be the single and most important accomplishment that you can achieve. Every project that you pursue will be in alignment with your purpose. You will feel alive and invigorated, each and every day. As you focus on what you want to be remembered for, you'll see yourself as the person that you want to become.

That is the very least you can do in your life is to figure out what you hope for. And the most you can do is live inside that hope. Not admire it from a distance but live right in it, under its roof.
— Barbara Kingsolver

Exercise: Can you describe the action that you see yourself doing, the type of person or organization that you want to work for or serve? Describe the goals that you want to create within that company or organization. Give yourself three items to shoot for in the next three months.

_____

_____

_____

_____

_____

_____

_____

_____

_____

_____

_____

_____

_____

_____

Does This Bring You Closer To your Purpose?

Small goals don't move men, they just irritate and annoy them.
— **Donald Trump**

Make your goals big and strong. Allow them to move you. Fill yourself with enthusiasm and let it be part of you. Integrate purpose into your daily life. Know that you're going to create each and every day an action that'll get you closer to making a difference in your life. Know your purpose. Ask yourself: does this bring me closer to my purpose? Do these goals serve my ultimate purpose? The higher purpose in your life doesn't mean that you have to quit your job or that you can't do what you enjoy doing as a hobby. You can live on purpose no matter what you do. However, in this case you will be involved emotionally only if the goal grabs your attention.

Not being connected to your purpose in life will cause you to be less than you were meant to be. There is no failure except for the person who no longer continues to move toward his purpose. There is no obstacle that is too big when you are on purpose. There is no challenge that is too powerful for you to overcome when on purpose. The most important job that you have is discovering that you're connected with what your purpose is. And, when you are on that purpose, when it's a raging, roaring, burning desire for you, then you're lit on fire. Every day you take a step forward, you will feel more alive than you ever have before. The first step to charting the course is for you to go on a quest to discover what it is that you were put here for? What is your assignment/purpose? What activities will you partake in daily that will enrich your soul and make a difference for you and the rest of the world? Complete the exercises in this section and obtain complete clarity on what that purpose is.

Construct the optimal you! Just imagine how great your life will be when it's injected with the passion of your purpose every day, to have the ability to choose your activities and goals and align it with your career. When your dominant strengths are coupled with what you love, you will ignite passion instantaneously. You're going to greet each and every day with harmony, joy and wonderment. Life will truly be magical.

Exercises:

- What would get you jazzed? What action would get you jazzed? Are you a promoter? Are you somebody who likes to listen, influence, inspire, communicate, demonstrate, discover, empower, acknowledge or entertain? Put all those words in a list of actions to be chosen from below:

_____

_____

_____

_____

_____

_____

_____

_____

_____

_____

_____

_____

_____

_____

- **Creating a passionate, purposeful future.** One way for you to discover what you're truly passionate about is to take real notice of what you like. In this exercise, you want to start to list all of the things that you like. You should have a column of things you don't like or don't want. We seem to have an easier time determining what we don't like or want. This way you can list the opposite of what *you don't want* and then focus on what *you do want*, creating energy and attention upon those results.

Likes/love	Dislikes/hate
_____	_____
_____	_____
_____	_____
_____	_____
_____	_____
_____	_____
_____	_____
_____	_____
_____	_____
_____	_____
_____	_____

- **What is the end result you want to create?** Think about the finish line, the end result that you want to create. Is it to empower, improve, to help others be healthier, give people security, freedom, love, acceptance, health, vitality, educate, serve others, make a contribution, help others believe in themselves? Help others be entertained, laugh, feel joy? Enter your words that represent to you the "End Results" that you want in your life. "I know I will be happy and fulfilled when..." and enter the emotional states you need.

End Results: I will be happy and fulfilled when...

<u>Examples</u>:
I am respected
I am honest
I am cheerful
I am secure

_____

_____

_____

_____

- Now, create a column of your positive traits and your areas of improvement. List them below.

Positive Traits   **Areas of Improvement**

_____   _____

_____   _____

_____   _____

_____   _____

_____   _____

_____   _____

_____   _____

_____   _____

_____   _____

- **Put together a list of all the things you love and match them with all the things that are your strengths.**

I love to...   I am good at...

_____   _____

_____   _____

_____   _____

_____   _____

_____   _____

_____   _____

_____   _____

Then, see whether they fit in a category in a particular field. It will help you to know what you're truly passionate about. For instance, if you're not athletic yet you're somebody who is into health and nutrition, you may find yourself becoming a personal trainer or nutritionist. If you're somebody who happens to be very articulate, intelligent and a great communicator, then maybe you're going to be a debater or a public speaker. Think about the things that you're good at, passionate about and what you're naturally strong at. Combine them and come up with a list of possible fields that you would love to partake in. Don't worry if your mind says "No, I'm not good at that," or "I never was good at that." It may just be a belief that somebody else planted in your Garden (mind). My father didn't like to dance and always said he had two left feet. He said that I inherited his rhythm which was awful. I never felt inclined to dance. In fact, I was scared and embarrassed and only danced after having a few drinks. However, I learned with time that dancing is not right or wrong — it's about moving yourself freely, like a child without inhibitions. I decided to enroll in dance lessons and was slow to learn initially, but with some good instructions I realized that dancing is a wonderful expression of self-love. I gave myself the freedom to move and groove wherever and whenever I decided to. You are not others! Trust your heart and then just start!

- Practice answering the above questions to dig below the surface. Write down in your journal the answer to those questions. Do so for at least seven days. Go for it. Don't settle and let that voice inside of you that said, "I don't have time, money or resources. It wasn't meant to be" hold you back. Don't let that voice own you. It doesn't own you. It's only programming from the past that hasn't served you. It's time for you to step through that voice to the other side, the real you. Claim the victory of being in the mindset of those that succeed at mastering their inner game and achieving the results you dream of. Do your assignment and then go on to the next chapter.

Summary

- Everyone was put here for a reason. Your job is to discover what it is!
- You will feel most alive when you are doing what you love.
- Statistics reveal that millionaires become millionaires not so much because they love money but because when they do what they love, they radiate and shine. Money becomes the by-product of passionately following your purpose.
- Discovering your MVP, you must remove the old conditioning that you're not worthy of pursuing your personal passion.
- You must dust off the negative beliefs that your life has piled on you to keep you from believing that all your dreams are possible.
- Action Option: For the next seven days journal for 10 minutes before bedtime.
  1. Each day answer the following questions, digging in to your unconscious mind.

2. Take a deep breath and relax.
3. Answer these questions prior to sleeping:
   - What is my purpose, mission and reason for being here?
   - What do I love?
   - What am I passionate about?
   - When am I happiest?
   - What would I do if I knew I couldn't fail?
   - How do I want to be remembered? For what?

Now you know who you have been. Now you know what you want... your MVP. Now you need a plan on how to get there. So let's create the identity of the optimal you! Because you will behave congruently with the way you see yourself when you declare that you are a certain way (your new optimal self), you will behave more like that person. Understanding the impact that our beliefs have on our identities is the next step.

Chapter 3:
Creating Your Optimal Identity

People take on the nature, the habits, and the power thought of those with whom they associate most.

— **Henry Ford**

Beliefs

Where do your beliefs come from? **They come from your past.** From your teachers, environment, peers and colleagues — people who influence you through one of three vehicles:

1) **What you've heard**. *Children are meant to be seen and not heard.* So you start to believe it's important for you to not speak. You become very quiet. Now, you're a little introverted, because there is a benefit, payoff, love or appreciation attached to your being quiet. Remember, the unconscious mind is trained for survival. Its mechanism is trained to avoid things that are painful and to direct us toward things that are pleasurable.

2) **What you've seen**. Parents yelling at each other then ignoring each other. Parents drinking heavily, cheating, exaggerating, lying or behaving in a dishonorable manner. Their behavior caused you pain and you are determined not to be like them. So you'll be quiet. Quiet is safe.

3) **What you feel, your Triple E™**. Parents shaming you, telling you to apologize or be quiet because you're embarrassing them. You are hurt. Traumatized. You won't forget the lesson. If you are quiet, this won't happen again.

These vehicles manifest in various ways. A child may become troublesome at school to gain the attention of their parents. This happens all the time. A child may be given praise for excelling in a sport and then uses that as their vehicle to meet their need for attention and love. They now believe that if they excel in sports, they are worthy of attention and love. This could cause them to develop self-discipline, persistence and make them into a hard worker.

Empowering Beliefs

You've chartered a course. You understand your passion and your purpose. You know your mission and you have your vision. Everything is possible for people who have strong beliefs. Beliefs have fuelled many above and beyond difficult challenges. There is no question that strong beliefs are required to achieve great success.

Later on, you will learn how to visualize your future and how to enhance your beliefs through imagination and visualization, creating a vision so exciting it's almost tangible. Many have done this before.

Comedian and actor Martin Short is a prime example. He practiced visualization regularly as a young child fantasizing about being an entertainer. He would do the Martin Short Show. He sang and interviewed people and played fake applause after each glowing performance. He even went so far as to type up his show's guest list for the *TV Guide* listing. His success now speaks for itself.

Beliefs, when spoken regularly out loud or internally through the process of autosuggestion, visualization and affirmations, are strengthened. Let's face it — **any belief, good or bad, is strengthened by repetition**. If we believe that we are good singers, good communicators, or smart, we will look for situations to re-confirm those beliefs. When virtually any situation arises where we don't have the answer, we rely on blaming ourselves for not being enough. The objective is to

think about the beliefs that will get us to where we want to go.
Here are some examples:

Youth is strength... age is wisdom.

Everyone has 24 hrs. I can achieve whatever I
want with passion, purpose and a vision.

We live in a world of free information.
I can learn whatever I choose.

The universe made me for a unique purpose.

By giving it my best effort I will deserve it all.

Life is about abundance. There is plenty for everyone.

I believe that I can.

I will get what I expect; I will expect the best and get it.

There is only winning and learning!

I can achieve whatever I want as long as
I am committed and creative.

I believe that I am responsible for everything in my life.

I am at the cause of everything in my life.

Nobody can make me feel any way without my consent.

Nothing has meaning until I give it a meaning!

Life is beautiful! I attract abundance into my life.

Though people mean well, they often give us negative beliefs based on what *they* were taught. They are unaware that what they were taught had a negative impact on *them*. We now live in a different time. We have access to more information and have better control of the perception of our beliefs.

Our mission here is **to identify the beliefs that are weak and to replace them with beliefs that are strong.** This isn't a simple process, but you can work on doing it by changing your references that support each belief. In other words, question each belief that doesn't serve you until you create enough doubt. Replace that disempowering belief with an empowering one. There is a process that we go through in one of my peak performance seminars that allows us to radically shake the certainty of those negative beliefs, by undermining their power and weakening the hold they have on us.

In other words, if we go to **our garden,** some of those disempowering beliefs (or weeds, if you will) have huge roots and there is a great amount of energy that was invested in supporting them. Even though the fruit that they give us is poisonous, it is still part of our identity. So we support and even defend these disempowering beliefs. You are going to need to **uproot** them and make sure they're exterminated. Follow this by **replanting** some empowering beliefs and **nurture** those new beliefs in order to create some powerful new trees in our garden. This experience is life-altering.

Surviving A Concentration Camp

Victor Frankel believes that there was a purpose in his survival of a concentration camp. That purpose was for him to tell his story. This belief pushed him through his incredible survival in circumstances of great pain and torture. Armed with this belief, he survived others who were wiped out by their own thoughts. He wrote *Man's Search for Meaning* after having survived seven years in a concentration camp in Auschwitz. He said that many men focused on the evil and pain that was around them, and understandably so. All those poisonous trees were everywhere causing people to give up and die, while others like him, chose to focus on the empowering meanings of that horrific experience. As difficult as it was, he managed to find a small seed of hope and determination. By focusing on what he desired he was able to grow this seed into a tree of faith. Using his imagination, he visualized reuniting with his wife as often as possible. Those seeds of thought grew into trees with deep roots and grew stronger over time. In spite of being battered by the Gestapo, he nurtured his positive thoughts and survived. Many a guard tried to smash the life out of his hope. Yet his faith nourished these trees of hope. Through determination he was able to nurture these thoughts and energized them with his beliefs. He would repeatedly nurture these thoughts through imagination and faith, and he survived circumstances that defied what most people would be able to endure today. He *believed* that the last of human freedoms is to choose one's attitude. It is our responsibility to choose our destinies through the power of our own minds — to choose our mindsets and our beliefs. It is our responsibility to decide the best and most powerful meanings that we can attach to the events in our life.

Fail Your Way To Success

If you want to increase your success rate, double your failure rate.
— **Thomas Watson, Sr.**

Learn to attach an empowering meaning to the events in your life. What beliefs can you attach to failure to get yourself excited? Rather than discouragement or frustration, discover the experiences that make you stronger. The power of focus will dictate your mindset, which will determine whether you achieve incredible results, or whether you just have an incredibly pathetic story to tell others. Successful people learn the power of focus and how to find empowering beliefs to keep them moving forward. They realize that each event carries within it the seed of opportunity. Do you think about all the things that can go wrong with your day or are you eager to try new things, knowing that they carry the seeds of growth, experience and possibility?

It's time to change your focus, ask better questions and start to shape your identity. You can take responsibility for your life. You stand at the gate of your garden and anyone who tries to enter and plant weeds will be kindly escorted away by your new and improved identity. Others will try to plant poisonous trees in your garden by telling you that you can't do it or you are not intelligent enough, etc. They'll attempt to plant some disempowering beliefs in your mind and tell you that you're not smart enough. In many cases, it's not because they want you to fail, it's because they don't want you to be hurt like they were by disappointment and rejection when they tried to live their dreams. They will try to talk you out of going for it. Do not listen. Engage in your dream. They fear being at a lower level than you and nobody likes that feeling. For many, it is easier to pull others down and away from their dreams than it is for them to step up and pursue their own dreams through growth and uncertainty.

Everyone is ignorant, only in different subjects.

— **Will Rogers**

Eventually your garden (identity) will develop a reputation and the empowering trees (beliefs) will be so big that the negative trees (disempowering beliefs) will know that there is no more room for them to grow. The shade of the big trees (those big, strong beliefs) will not allow them to grow. Your strong beliefs will now become convictions. When tested and knocked around by life, you will see that you have developed the ability to starve the weeds (your fears) and feed your dreams. By doing what is difficult in life it will eventually become easier and easier. This is how you build your self-esteem. Sooner or later, you will be planting beliefs about yourself that you had no idea you even knew you could grow. You will try and succeed at singing, dancing, acting, flying a plane, opening a business, public speaking and inspiring others to grow their dreams. You will see the garden of your life is limitless. You can decide what you will nurture and how you will grow it.

Henry Ford said it best: "Whether you think you can or can't, you're right."

Some weeds grow large and are poisonous. The beliefs we have that disempower us, like "I'm lazy, a procrastinator, not smart enough, ugly, short, dumb, I can't sing," are the poison. If we focus on those negative weeds, they will grow into larger trees. <u>You get what you focus on in your life</u>, whether you want it or not. If you focus on being a loser, think about being a loser and look for all the times you've been a loser, you're going to act like a loser.

We need to start shaping our identities consciously with care and thought. I became aware that I had an identity that wasn't supporting me and I kept on referring to myself as someone who wasn't funny. So when I was in situations with friends, I kept on telling myself, *I'm not funny, I don't know what to say*. Guess what? I didn't know what to say. Your brain is going to build the results that you command of it. (Recall the Captain's Crew metaphor.)

Saying It's So
*What you say is so
you begin to sow
and you will become just so.*

Then I developed a Power Identity Statement — an autosuggestion (something that you say to yourself repeatedly as an affirmation or a dialogue that you have with yourself). You repeat it throughout the day; you read it morning, noon and night. However quickly you desire to transform your identity is how often you need to read or say it to yourself. You can even record it on a tape and listen to it again in the car. My particular phrase included the fact that I was as playful as a four-year-old. I would say that again and again. Given certain situations, I would ask myself, what would Jim Carey or Robin Williams do here? Or what would a four-year-old boy do in this situation? I would act as if I was that particular individual. That's what expanding a new identity is all about. It's a process that takes a little bit of time, but with a bit of practice you can get there. Soon, I was doing imitations and was making funny faces. I was transforming my own identity. My personality went from somebody who, in most situations, felt that he wasn't adequate or funny, to being someone who takes great joy in clowning around, doing imitations and being spontaneous and childlike. I'll tell you something: **The quality of my life has dramatically changed through this one process**.

It may sound a little bit extreme, but I believe that you're somebody who picked up this book because you wanted to make some shifts, changes, and to learn. I want to give you the best possible tools for you to do that. The purpose of my life is to help people tap into the part of them that hasn't yet been expressed. It pains me to see people who don't have the resources and tools that allow them to really enjoy their lives.

Writing Out The Optimal You In Detail

The shift in identity is a process of writing out who you want to become. By repeating it and acting as if you are that person already, you will become that person. **In other words, saying "I am** playful, funny, generous, caring, I am..." will move you closer to behaving the way you want to be. It doesn't mean you're not enough. It just means that you can reach more of your potential by knowing what your potential is! Every day we're headed somewhere new. Why not choose a destination of your choice, rather than just driving around in circles? Decide on who you want to be and how you plan on broadcasting your character to the world.

You're going to write down in your journal, *I am* ... and write down all the adjectives that explain who you want to become more of. Remember: this is a book about expanding your comfort zone or identity. This is a book about growing so that the inner part of you can expand and you can connect with your passion every day. Remember: **life is a journey, not a destination.** The fact that you've gotten where you are is wonderful. Acknowledge everything you've done in your past and let it serve your future. But don't stop growing!

I have been through many failures. I failed in the restaurant business. I've lost tons of money in different business ventures, on the stock market and have been in failed relationships. They were all opportunities for me to gain experience. I don't begrudge them. I look at them and am grateful for the fact that I have learned from them. So why not glean the learning from your past?

Identities

Here are some sample identities:

1) <u>**Career Identity**</u>. I am a fantastic... peak transformational coach/trainer, gifted to obtain results rapidly and playfully. CEO of several companies (each in its own right) massively successful, bringing value to the marketplace. A top negotiator, shrewd judge of character and an attractor of opportunity, I have an elite ability to assemble key staff in all of my companies. Master communicator with business partners and clients. Compassionate and respectful to the needs and desires of those who seek my guidance.

2) <u>**Emotional Identity**</u>. I am... fun-loving, grateful, growing, dynamic, inspirational, energetic, cheerful, spontaneous, outrageous, positive and playful, spiritual, intelligent, loving, guided, happy, healthy, wealthy, creative, courageous and a blessed soul.

3) <u>**Health Identity**</u>. I am... ripped, an athletic machine. Constantly honoring my body with water, healthy foods made up of at least 70% greens. I have fantastic posture, great hygiene and the discipline to exercise daily. Movement equals magic. I am playful and a child at heart. I love sports and excel at everything I do,

because I give it my all and I never give up. It's about the journey, not the destination.

Now fill in your eight gardens with words that resonate well with you and cause you to feel excited and alive.

1) You can refer to the first exercise we did where you captured words, which you highlighted and wanted to keep (because they served you).

2) Insert any word that reflects something you would like to be more of. Perhaps consistent, reliable, joyful... enter as many as you like. (It took me months to develop some, so have fun with it!) It doesn't have to be perfect as you're just starting. Beginning may be the hardest part, but once you start, the benefits remain.

3) Think of your heroes or people who exemplify the traits you like. Write them down.

4) Draw from Chapter 2. What do you like and what are you passionate about?

Put these all together on the garden provided or go to www.rockthomas.com and download blank forms to fill in your optimal identity. It is a work in progress. Add to it, and you will see it grow based on your values and desires. Even if you feel you'll never achieve it, enter the words and watch the **magic!**

Summary

- Use power of questions to change your focus. (What's great about this? What can I learn?)
- You can change the meaning of any event by simply asking to yourself, "What's the best meaning I can attach to this" and "How will it energize me forward?"
- Your garden/identity is built upon what you focus on; who you become depends greatly upon the habit of focus and choice. Focus on the beliefs you desire to grow and they will become towering Redwood trees, leaving no room for weeds.
- **Continue to write out the words that begin with "I am**

..." and form your optimal self. Put in all the adjectives that will explain who you want to become. Once you've written it out, repeat it again and again. You will feel a shift. Your energy levels will transform. You will find yourself feeling more and more fulfilled. What you say, you will become one day! Saying it so *does* make it so!

IDENTITY   **I AM...**

Emotions   ... _____

_____

_____

_____

_____

_____

_____

_____

_____

_____

_____

Spiritual   ... _____

_____

_____

_____

_____

_____

_____

_____

_____

_____

_____

Family &
Friends

… _____

_____

_____

_____

_____

_____

_____

_____

_____

_____

_____

Intimate
Relationships

… _____

_____

_____

_____

_____

_____

_____

_____

_____

_____

_____

Career

… _____

_____

_____

_____

_____

_____

_____

_____

_____

_____

_____

Financial ... _____
_____
_____
_____
_____
_____
_____
_____
_____
_____
_____
_____

Hobbies ... _____
_____
_____
_____
_____
_____
_____
_____
_____
_____
_____
_____

Health ... _____
_____
_____
_____
_____
_____
_____
_____
_____
_____
_____
_____

Chapter 4:
Closing the Gap

Now that you know who you are and where you came from, it's time to **close the gap from where you are to where you want to be**. This process of closing the gap will be the final stroke in creating your optimal self — the person you were meant to be. In order to integrate this new identity into your nervous system and help you to behave consistently at your best, I have created a menu of ways for you to perform at your personal best. This is a process of re-programming who you are by over writing who you have been with who you want to be. By applying all of these methods, you will become the person who you ideally would like to be, your fate is in your hands and (more specifically) in the words that you feed your mind daily.

1) <u>Read out loud </u>what you have written in each one of your gardens everyday or as often as you can. Your transformation will be in direct proportion to how much time you spend with the new self image that you have created for yourself. You will not change if you do not focus on the words that describe the new you.

2) <u>Reading them </u>just before you go to bed is very effective as you will anchor them into your thoughts and dreams and allow your body to bathe in them. This will stimulate change at an unconscious level.

3) <u>Record them </u>on a tape or CD and then listen to them in the car and at home as much as you can. This will increase your awareness of how you need to show up in your life. If you hear yourself saying to yourself that you hydrate your body with at least eight bottles of water every day and you hear it over and over again,

you will find yourself reaching for water more often.

This is how advertising works – the repetition of suggestions will eventually result in an action being taken. Create the proper ad for yourself and then play it again and again until you are programmed to take action consistently.

4) <u>Work out</u> and repeat the identity statements you have written for each one of your gardens. You may choose one or two per day until you memorize them. Saying them while you are moving will anchor the message more powerfully into your nervous system. Motion creates momentum. When you speak and move, you are more able to convince yourself of the words that you are using.

   Consider when you are in a heated telephone discussion — is it not true that you need to get up and pace? Sitting down does not give you the focus or energy required to get the best of yourself. Instead of watching mindless TV while running on the treadmill you can now focus on who you are working on becoming by repeating the words in your mind or out loud. Whether you call them mantras or affirmations, they are simply the words that create the thoughts that create the emotions in your body. Dynamic movement creates dynamic change. How rapidly you would like to create this change depends upon how much effort you will put into changing the old programming for the new.

5) <u>Be Bold.</u> Talk about the changes you have planned in your life with those who can support you. They will be your cheerleaders when you are frustrated by reminding you of your "word" and your "rewards." They will be the ones who are your mentors. They will be comfortable with your future. These are the type of people who are above average and who will pull you forward and give you some pain if you drop your standards too often. Like a good athlete has a coach,

we, too, need coaches along the way to remind us of what we already know, yet sometimes forget to do. Spend time with as many people as you can who have already achieved the results that you want to achieve. Like osmosis, they will rub off on you and you will become the company that you keep.

6) <u>Use the naysayers as catalysts.</u> There will be many people who will try to keep you back. They will tell you that you cannot achieve those lofty goals or that you are just not "that way." **Prove them wrong**. Not so much to be right, but rather to be a role model to them for what is possible. That change can occur with the right environment and tools. Life is 90% negative, so get used to swimming against the current. Otherwise you will never make it! Learn to be grateful for the opponents that are always there on your trek to a great life!

7) <u>Act *as if*,</u> which simply means that if you were the person you want to be, how would you behave? If you were a millionaire, how would you handle your money and investments? What kind of a negotiator would you be? If you are thinking that you can be irresponsible, start flying first class, and running up your credit cards then you are missing the point. By not having any guidelines or rules of conduct, you leave yourself open to any kind of behavior. Ask yourself how the people you model would make this decision, react, or take action. Then implement your self-discipline to make take the same action and make it happen.

8) <u>Pictures are worth a 1000 words</u>. Post your identity statements and pictures that exemplify who you want to become around your house, in your car, on your computer — wherever you spend time. This will help saturate you into your new identity. You can also post some of your goals to help compel you to achieve them.

My role models saturated themselves and became masters in their fields. Elvis Presley had music in every room in the house. No wonder he became a genius in that field – he bathed in it all the time. You are what you eat — mentally and visually. So fill your surroundings with the sights and sounds of success!

9) <u>Spend time</u> with whom you desire to become in as many ways as you can. You will become this person with much less effort than you might imagine. That is not to say there will be no effort. But the power of your identity and the desire for you to remain consistent with the way that you see yourself will become a dominant force, pulling you to your ultimate and optimal self each and every day!

Practice makes perfect and repetition is the skill of success. You are either feeding your dreams or feeding your fears. It really comes down to what you choose to focus on in your life. If you want it all, then it will require some effort. It will, however, be worth your while. So take your new identity and use these guidelines to close the gap as fast as you can! I hope you reap the rewards for all of your efforts quickly and with pleasure.

Printed in the United States
67006LVS00004BB/268-504

9 781425 982706